A Boy's War

by David J. Michell

OMF BOOKS

A BOY'S WAR

© 1988 Overseas Missionary Fellowship (*formerly China Inland Mission*)
Published by OMF International (IHQ) Ltd.
2 Cluny Road, Singapore 259570, Republic of Singapore.

First published 1988
Second printing 1990
Third printing 1997

ISBN 9971-972-71-9

To my parents, Walter and Reba Michell,
my sisters, Joyce and Joan, and brother Brian
—though out of sight for much of this story,
they were seldom out of mind.

The student huts that became home
to whole families when the
Courtyard of the Happy Way
became Weihsien Concentration Camp
under Japanese occupation.

Drawing by Eileen Bazire.

The sketch above and those by Helen Hulse Fox
in *A Boy's War* are used courtesy of
the Chefoo Schools Association.

Contents

Preface

Many of the following boyhood memories and experiences have been told in little segments over these past forty years, but somehow the task of threading the whole story together in response to many requests kept eluding me.

My wife Joan, more than anyone else, has been the most patient listener and has helped me in working through the feelings and meaning of these experiences. Our four children—Robyn, Heather, Ken, and Judith—have been familiar with most of the adventures from their earliest years. At one time, in fact, I recorded my story incognito, under the title of "The Boy X from China," and Joan would play an episode each night before the children went to bed when I was away on missionary travels.

I am grateful for the Overseas Missionary Fellowship's giving me time for sabbatical study, and to Dr. Timothy M. Warner of Trinity Evangelical Divinity School for allowing me to write my story as part of my Doctor of Missiology degree program.

When I came to put pen to paper, I found it hard to get started because my emotions were so often near the surface.

At Christmas time 1985, as I sat enjoying excerpts from *The Messiah* at our home church, Spring Garden Baptist in Willowdale (Toronto), Ontario, I was startled to read in the church bulletin that Handel had written the music for *The Messiah* in only twenty-three days. Then and there I said to myself, *February has twenty-eight days; I'm going to write my story*.

Through the long winter days of February 1986 my mind tunneled its way to the places and events of far-off China. A silent and faithful supporter throughout the months in the whole enterprise was Penny, our golden retriever, who sat at or on my feet under the desk into the early morning hours.

I am indebted to many for their help in this venture and want to express my thanks to them all: Many of my Chefoo teachers and CIM missionaries shared with me their reminiscences; Norman Cliff, Langdon Gilkey, Rene Rouse, Laurance Tipton, Gordon Martin, Raymond de Jaegher, and others provided invaluable sources through their books or other writings.

Numerous helpful sugestions that have come from D. V. Gonder, Krysia Lear, Margaret Bunting, Bill and Vera Tyler, Isabel Taylor, and others have been most gladly included. The skillful and generous editing of Alice Poynor and Fay Goddard has brought the book to its present form, and for this I am very thankful.

Without the dedicated and enthusiastic typing of the manuscript in its various stages, this project would never have come to fruition, and I want sincerely to thank Joy Wilton, Marilyn Hodges, and Larry Seguin.

My hope is that this story will not lead the reader to the conclusion that everything turned out well for everyone who was interned during World War II. Some, I know, still suffer from the effects of the separation and the hardships.

The book and film, *Empire of the Sun,* portrayed powerfully the story of a boy in his attempts "to survive in a world at war [in which] he must find a strength greater than all the events that surround him." My story from Weihsien—and that also of others in the camp, as well as at Lungwha—is a testimony to the presence and power of God through His help and through people. Experiencing this presence and power turned what could have been nothing but tragedy and trauma into triumph.

David J. Michell
March 1988
Toronto

Foreword

Are they really compatible—God's design for the family and His call to world evangelism? Far from being merely a question for classroom debate, this is a question for which potential missionaries and supporting churches increasingly demand answers. *A Boy's War* has some answers—not easy answers, but answers.

Given the breakdown of family life in Western countries—with rampant divorce, single parents, working mothers, absentee fathers, etc.—Christians are right to place fresh emphasis on God's plan for the home. Not surprisingly, parents preparing for missionary service struggle with guilt about the legitimacy of taking children overseas. Many wrestle with the hard issues of how they can both serve in their missionary calling and at the same time meet the needs of their family.

Missionary societies know that this is an important area. Enabling families to cope overseas, with the inevitable demands and risks that missionary life entails, absorbs considerable time, energy, and expense. The whole matter has, in fact, become a major inter-mission concern and has spawned a number of helpful programs and resources in recent years to assist families to face cross-cultural living and ministry.

And yet there are times in the life of a missionary family when things don't go as planned and when circumstances seem out of control. Should the risks to our family keep us from moving ahead? Where should we draw the line between responsible action for the welfare of the family and obedience to the claims of the Great Commission?

Our Lord warned that true discipleship would not be without cost, nor obedience to the Great Commission without its price to the family. We need to keep this perspective. Whatever the cost, however, I am convinced—both as a parent and as a counselor/friend to hundreds of other missionary families—that God's design and care for the family and His call to world evangelism are not incompatible.

David Michell's experiences of life as a missionary kid in a worst-case scenario bring a sober realism to any discussion on MK issues. They also bring encouragement. For through the trauma of war, separation from parents, and deprivation we see God's faithfulness and His ability to meet the deepest needs of His children.

What is amazing is to see how the author not only survived his ordeal, but in time he himself served as a missionary in Japan, with all the implications for his own young family, and today is an active proponent of families in missions. Circumstances which could have made David bitter and resentful God used to mold character and to create a bold dependence upon Him.

David Michell's story is powerful and moving because it deals with real life and the tough questions life brings. This book is not only entertaining, sometimes horrifying, and always inspirational—it carries an important practical message for all who face the apparent risks of obedience to Christ.

Dr. Daniel W. Bacon
U.S. Director
OMF International
Littleton, Colorado

Introduction

David Michell, my colleague and one-time Chefoo schoolmate and fellow internee in Weihsien, was born in China and did not leave until nearly into his teens. *A Boy's War* is David's account of his childhood years, beginning with the tumultuous Warlord Era and climaxing in a Japanese concentration camp in occupied China during World War II. This is not a chronicle of atrocities, but an expansion of cherished childhood memories. The disruption of boarding school life by internment is seen almost as a three-year cub scout camp.

The heroes of David's boyhood live again—Eric Liddell, the "Flying Scotsman"; "Pa" Bruce, the Headmaster; "Goopy" Martin, the legendary Latin teacher; and Tipton and Hummel, who escaped from the Japanese concentration camp and consequently set up the most ingenious underground communication system. In the absence of his own parents, these heroes filled an important surrogate role. Clearly the quality of the Christian character of most of David's heroes contributed significantly to David's own spiritual development and to his ability to cope with the trauma of separation and wartime China.

A Boy's War is also the chronicle of David's early pilgrimage. Amid the excitement and drama of earth-shaking events the reader sees the plan of God traced in the life of a lad. The extension of that is seen in the years David served in Japan and in the impact of his life in Canada today.

Dr. James H. Taylor III
Consulting Director, Chinese Ministries
OMF International
Hong Kong

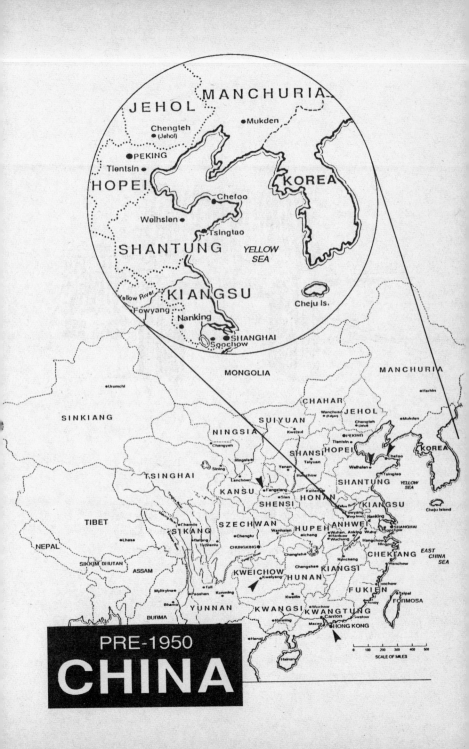

PRE-1950
CHINA

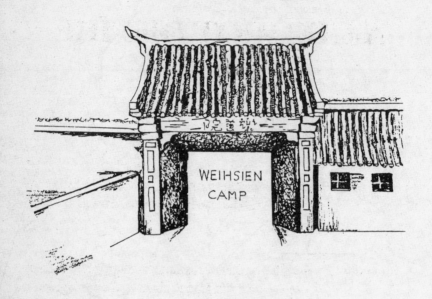

WEIHSIEN
CAMP

The gate to the "Courtyard of the Happy Way"
that became Weihsien Concentration Camp.

Drawing by Judith Michell

Chapter 1

A CHARIOT OF FIRE

"But at my back I always hear
Time's winged chariot hurrying near."
—Andrew Marvell, *To His Coy Mistress*

*T*he runners crouched in starting position, tensed for the signal that would spring them down the track.

It was late August, 1944. I was eleven, one boy in a whole school of missionaries' children interned under the Japanese. Home was Weihsien (Weixian) Concentration Camp in Shantung (Shandong) Province, North China.

That sports day on the playing field was a speck of glitter in the dull monotony of camp life. The youngest children ran first, then we juniors, pounding down the track barefoot, in hand-me-down shorts and shirts. Yelling and laughing, we slapped each others' backs as we finished the course.

Then, as the veterans' race prepared to start, a hush distilled over the crowd. Our eyes shifted to the chairman of the Camp Recreation Committee, who was starting well behind the others as a voluntary handicap. "He can never make up that distance!" gasped a boy beside me.

"He can too! He will, just wait!" I hissed back.

Down the track they came. Middle-aged runners, weakened by the rigors and poor food of camp life, puffed and panted their way onward in response to our cheers. Then, unbelievably, the runner in rear position surged powerfully forward, arms flailing wildly, head thrown back. Out ahead now, he pushed for the finish line. He did it! One great, wild chorus of cheers nearly drowned out the judge's voice, "Eric Liddell wins the veterans' event!"

"I knew he could do it! He always wins!" The Olympic gold medalist, whose 400-meter win had made him a legend twenty years earlier, had won our hearts long before this day as he shared our prison experience. We basked in an aura of Olympic glory as—cheering, chanting, chattering—we surrounded our hero.

We wanted to stretch the excitement, squeeze out every drop of enjoyment of this day. All too soon the reality of our grim world crept back as the late afternoon sun elongated the shadows of barbed wire and watchtowers that hemmed us in.

Already more than a year had passed since our school had been marched in under guard to join the rest of the prisoners. There were over two hundred of us, children of missionaries, separated by war from parents who were working in inland China, in regions not yet taken over by the Japanese. Business people, tourists, entertainers, and their families as well as children from other schools made up the rest of the prison population. More than a third of the internees, in fact, were children. For all of us life was confined within the high brick walls that ran around the Weihsien compound.

The Japanese guards, with bared bayonets, were never out of

sight by day, pacing along the foot of the forbidding gray walls or clustered at the main gates or corner searchlight towers. Even by night the searchlight beams—sweeping across the camp and over the deep trenches and coiled barbed wire— reminded us of the soldiers' presence. Across those trenches and outside those walls was the world we had once known.

*T*wo hundred miles to the northeast of Weihsien on the coast, lay the city of Chefoo (Yantai). Back in 1881 this seaside spot was chosen for a school for the children of missionaries of the China Inland Mission. It was as a student in this school that I had been captured and interned in Weihsien. It is at Chefoo that my story really begins. My parents were members of the China Inland Mission.

The founder of the mission, James Hudson Taylor, had arrived in China in 1854.[1] Dismayed to find most of the missionaries living in the foreign concessions in Shanghai rather than out among the people, he adopted the dress and hair style of the Chinese and moved inland to unreached areas of the country. Six years later, he took his burden for China's unreached millions back to England.

In June of 1865 Hudson Taylor, trusting God to give him and provide for "24 willing, skillful laborers,"[2] opened a bank account with £10 ($20) in the name of the China Inland Mission. The following year, on May 26, aboard the sailing ship *Lammermuir*, he and his wife and four children left Liverpool with the first band of missionaries of the CIM.

[1]Dr. and Mrs. Howard Taylor, *Hudson Taylor in Early Years*, Vol. 1 of 2-vol. biography (Philadelphia, China Inland Mission, first printed 1911. Reprinted 1988, Overseas Missionary Fellowship, Singapore).
[2] A. J. Broomhall, *Hudson Taylor & China's Open Century: If I Had a Thousand Lives, Book III* (London: Hodder & Stoughton and the Overseas Missionary Fellowship, 1982), p. 436.

By the time of my story the China Inland Mission was the largest Protestant mission in China, having more than a thousand missionaries scattered across the whole expanse of China, many in the most remote areas. Our family was living in Kweiyang (Guiyang), the capital of Kweichow (Guizhou) province. My parents had joined the mission from Australia in 1930 and, after a seven-year term in Shensi (Shaanxi) in the north, were now working in the southwest.

In the China of those years the only way for most children of missionaries to get a good education in English was to go away to boarding school. Chefoo offered this opportunity. At Chefoo children of missionaries and a few sons and daughters of business people lived and studied together at the Preparatory School, the Boys' School, and the Girls' School, getting a truly Christian education for body, mind, and spirit.

So good was that education, in fact, that others, non-CIMers, wanted to take advantage of it too. Among the most illustrious North American graduates are Henry Luce of *Time* Magazine; playwright Thornton Wilder; Carrington Goodrich, for thirty-five years Professor of Chinese and Chairman of the Department of Asian Studies at Columbia University; Kenneth Taylor, Canada's former Deputy Minister of Finance; and Vivian Gonder, a Vice-President of Canadian National. In fact, in time Chefoo School became known as the best school east of the Suez Canal. The top class of the school, known as the Sixth Form, took the Oxford matriculation exams every June; and on graduation each student returned to his own homeland or to be with parents if home leave was imminent.

By late 1939 Chefoo School was nearly sixty years old, and I was six. It was my turn to be part of this time-honored pattern.

By the late 1930s, however, travel was no longer predictable—whether to go to school or to be united as a family at vacation time or to leave China for furlough. In that decade China under Chiang Kai-shek was battling insuperable odds in a civil war, the country weighed down with wide-spread banditry, monstrous corruption, and grinding poverty. From the southwest the Communists were relentlessly working their way northward on the "Long March." In the far northeast, following the Marco Polo Bridge incident in 1937, Japan's aggressive militarism began to cast a lengthening shadow of terror across China. At the best of times, travel to the nearest missionary was uncertain and could take many weeks. Now the internal turmoil made movement from one place to another even more hazardous.

Nevertheless, year by year from the widely scattered China Inland Mission outposts, tender six-year-olds, eased painfully from their parents' arms, made the long and often adventurous journey under the escort of missionaries to the far-off Chefoo School. Now it was my turn.

The Boy's School at Chefoo from 1896 to 1942.
Drawing by Helen Hulse Fox.

Chapter 2

MY TURN

"Parting is such sweet sorrow."
—William Shakespeare, *Romeo and Juliet*

*T*o get to Chefoo by the beginning of the next term on January 1, I had to leave on October the 8th, the day after my sixth birthday. For months my thoughts had never been very far away from that day and what lay ahead.

Everyone knew, including me, that just four years earlier a party of seventy-four Chefoo children en route to school after Christmas holidays were taken captive by pirates on the high seas. The pirates locked them up in their cabins and robbed them of some pocket money before the British Navy found the overdue ship, frightening off the pirates and escorting the ship safely to port. Since Chefoo children and their escorts were not harmed, their adventure was the envy of all the other children. The story gave me goose bumps.

Would such adventure be mine? I had mixed feelings about the possibility. One thing I knew was that at the end of the trip a reward would be to see my older sister, who had gone off to school a year before.

But to leave my parents and younger sister and my familiar world of the mission compound—with its moongate, my favorite secret hiding places and Chinese playmates—was a wrenching experience indeed.

I did feel glad to be leaving some things, however—things like the long, gray rats that seemed big enough to knock me over as they flip-flopped like giant carpet slippers across the courtyard in the dark; the crowds of local children and country people who would stand at the big wooden gateway and stare at the white child; and the low, drumming sound of the enemy planes, followed by the shrill air-raid siren and the frantic exodus of everyone to the nearest hills to hide behind the grave mounds. These things I would not miss at all.

The morning of departure dawned crisp and clear; the singsong calls of jostling street vendors mingled with the words and tears of farewell from the servants at the big wooden gate of the compound. Slowly the old mule cart with its wooden wheels began to draw away, with my parents, younger sister, and me perched precariously on the large steamer trunk loaded on the back. Somehow the big heavy trunk, filled with clothes for school for the next four years and all my earthly possessions, was like a sheet anchor as my little boat slipped away from its family moorings.

We reached the assembly point at the edge of the city, where a convoy of ramshackle trucks, which ran on anything from charcoal to gasoline, was being readied for transporting Red Cross supplies. One by one trucks backed up into position to be loaded. I was caught up in the excitement of the engines roaring, relieved to have a diversion from the furtive glances at my parents' anxious faces. Suddenly I saw the bright colors of a lumberjack's tartan shirt and a pair of legs dangling helplessly off the ground behind the truck that was being loaded. A truck had backed into a man, crushing him against another vehicle. Someone shouted an alarm, and as the driver frantically pulled clear, a limp body fell to the cold ground unconscious. It was Dr. Bob McClure, well-known Canadian United Church missionary, working at that time with the Red Cross. From that day on, the tartan and Canada are etched together indelibly in my memory.

The good-bye tears were postponed, and we returned home. Once more I took my football for another last kick and rode my bicycle with its training wheels round the compound paths. Even though word came a few days later that Dr. McClure had recovered, the truck's departure was delayed some weeks.

Eventually, however, all was ready. Farewells followed once more, cut short when our truck's engine coughed into action. As we took off with a lurch, I leaned forward, my eyes glued to the misting image of my family fading away in the distance. Tears welled up and spilled down my cheeks, falling onto the good-bye present I was clutching. And they continued to fall as I fumbled to open the package. Impatient to see what my parents had given me, I gave a final tear at the soggy wrappings, and there lay a brand new box of dominoes. I was delighted with them immediately. Hand-carved and beautifully finished, the dominoes had obviously been bought with some expense and care on the part of my parents. Still the tears welled up uncontrollably from deep down inside, splashing onto the game tiles on my lap, making puddles in the little number holes. I rubbed my fingers over the smooth blocks and did my best to comfort myself by counting the numbers of dots.

As we bounced around over the bumps and ruts of the dirt

road, I remembered the time I sat proudly atop my father's knee on the bed at home counting to ten for the first time. Other remembrances crowded in on each other and kept the tears streaming down my flushed cheeks. Only when tiredness overcame me did the tears subside, and I fell asleep, the dominoes clutched tightly in my hand.

By the time other "Prepites"—kids starting school for the first time—joined us on our six-week journey, I was one of the comforting party.

As it was wintertime, the roads were not the usual quagmire. Ice and snow, though, necessitated chains on the wheels as we crawled through the mountains.

We stayed a few nights in Anshun, where Dr. and Mrs. Edward Fish gave us hospitality, and Dr. Fish gave me my preschool medical examination at the Mission hospital. By this time the excitement of travel had long since dried my tears—so much so that my two lady missionary escorts, Miss Wilkinson and Miss Teegardin, later wrote to my parents, "David thinks it's all good fun." Their postcard of December 22, 1939, continued: "He is a grand little lad and a fine traveling companion. We feel very happy that you were willing to trust us with such precious cargo. He has decided not to hang one of my stockings on Christmas—he said he might get 'grown-up's' things. Instead he will hang two of his own. Everyone is thoroughly enjoying him. I trust you are not finding the days too lonely."

Lonely it may have been for our parents, especially when Christmas arrived. For us, though, the holiday was very happy in spite of our being away from home. We celebrated Christmas at Kunming, the capital of the neighboring province of Yunnan. The host and hostess at the Mission Home, used to the comings and goings of missionaries and children, took great care of us. We hung up our stockings and had a special

Christmas dinner. Then on the last day of the year our party was off again, this time by train.

I wiggled my way into my seat, crowding to see out the window, my belongings piled around me. Suddenly, a hand thrust in through the window grabbed my overcoat and pulled it out of the train just as we moved away from the platform.

I resented that loss. Not only was I cold, but when another coat was found for me, it was *a girl's coat!* Thankfully, at least the buttons were changed to the other side, because I had to wear it for several years.

Notes written en route tell of further travel hazards. "Today the Japanese flew over and bombed the railway about two hours from where we were. Planes flew over us and gave us a little scare. We are now waiting for the damaged track to be repaired so we can proceed. We may have to stay one night on the train. They tried for a bridge and hit the track at the mouth of a tunnel. David is out with Miss Teegarden gathering pieces of shrapnel. He is wonderfully excited—has found two pieces of his own. He has been very well and very good. He knows how to use his small head well . . . . We have been kept in great safety through many perils."

On January 5 we took ship from Haiphong (Hai Phong), the northern port of Indo-China, now Vietnam, and traveled right around the coast of China up to the camel's head promontory, where Chefoo is situated.

So bitterly cold was January 1940 that our boat became frozen in the bay, forcing us to travel to shore by rickshaw across the ice. My two pairs of knickerbockers, standard items on the boys' outfit list, did me little good. I was still freezing cold.

The school faced right onto the beach. Through the cold mist I could see a square, brick structure looming ever larger as our rickshaws approached. We crossed the road and passed the big

Boys' School building on our right and headed for the Prep School over to the left. Here our rickshaws creaked to a halt, and we climbed stiffly out. Shivering and scared, we huddled together, a small cluster in a strange, vast schoolyard. I was holding hands with Grace Allen, another six-year-old with whom I had traveled for most of the trip.

In tow of our missionary escorts we began to climb the wide steps up to the front doors. Two teachers with arms outstretched were coming towards us to welcome us. Suddenly the significance of what was happening swept over me. A surge of homesickness and pent-up resistance to the separation welled up inside. I took my stand on the steps, and I cried and cried. I turned to go back, but home was now two thousand miles and a six-week journey away. The more teachers coaxed and tried to guide me towards the door, the more I struggled to pull away. Eventually escorts and teachers won the day, and I was inside, unbloodied and uncowed.

Though the finality of the separation had come home to me and I was set to fight it, the prospect of seeing my older sister, Joyce, helped to weaken my antagonism. But the hoped-for solace was short-lived. Joyce, I was told, was in the sick bay; and worse than that, when I was led in to see her, I found her fast asleep. Small comfort here!

Notwithstanding, one of my early letters from school shows how quickly I settled in. "Chefoo May 27, 1940: Dear Grandma, Thank you for your nice letter and the hanky. I came here on a boat and train. I had a lovely time on the train. Joyce was in the sickroom when I came. One of the teachers took me in to see her. I like school very much. I like lessons and I like Sundays. All the days I like. With love from David M."

I could not have foreseen then what those days were to include for me.

CHEFOO

O Chefoo shore, so bare and wild.
Meet school for a poetic child;
Land of brown hills and blinding blasts,
Land of slow junks and swaying masts,
Land of my youth! What mortal hand
Can e'er untie the grateful band
That knits me to thy sunny strand?
As I review each well known scene,
Think what is now and what has been,
My soul would fain as once of yore
Stand on thy sunny shell-strewn shore.

—Anonymous

Chefoo Harbor with Chefoo School buildings in foreground.
Drawing by Helen Fox.

Chapter 3

JOYFUL
SCHOOL DAYS

"I have had playmates, I have had companions,
In my days of childhood, in my joyful school-days
—All, all are gone, the old familiar faces."
—Charles Lamb, *The Old Familiar Faces*

School life began for me in "Little End," the wing of the building where first and second graders were housed. These first two grades had the complicated names of Primary and Transition. A long way over, it seemed, at the other end of the Prep School building was Lower One and Upper One, or Grade Three and Grade Four. Though we were a very international mix from many Western countries, most of the teachers were British, and the system was predominantly after the English order. Coming from an Australian background, I did not find the adjustment difficult.

The story of Chefoo began with James Hudson Taylor, the founder of the CIM. In 1879 Hudson Taylor spent a heavy year preaching and traveling as well as bearing the responsibili-

ty of a growing group of workers. Exhausted and ill, he had
come to Chefoo, ordered by the doctor to rest before attempting
the many responsibilities that called him. There in such pleasant surroundings with the gentle sea breezes, his health improved rapidly. One afternoon as he walked on the beach with
Mr. and Mrs. Charles Judd, whose children were already of
school age, the thought came to him how very suitable the
gently sloping fields right ahead of him would be for a school
for the missionaries' children. Moreover it could serve as a ha-
ven where tired-out missionaries could rest.

What happened next would have been a surprise to anyone
without the childlike faith of Hudson Taylor. Moments later a
local farmer walked up to them and offered his bean field for
sale. Taylor had no doubts now—God was showing them his
purpose. In a short time a number of adjoining fields with a
gully and creek running through them were also purchased.
And God provided the timber, furnishings and fittings for the
Chefoo School from two shipwrecks. Thus the CIM Protestant
Collegiate School opened in 1881.

Seven years later the first principal and his successor had
both died, the former from illness and the latter from a mad dog
bite suffered while he was protecting some of the younger
children. Framed on the classroom wall some verses were
hung commemorating this latter leader's bravery:

> They bore him sadly to his early grave,
> On that green slope that fronts the restful tide,
> Their bright young faces awed to tearful calm
> —The lads for whom he died . . . .[1]

The Christian teaching and example of our teachers and those
who cared for us left its stamp on our lives. With what skill

[1] Stanley Houghton and others, *Chefoo* (London: China Inland Mission,
1931), pp. 28–36.

and memorable impact the story of *Pilgrim's Progress* came alive to us all! I found myself on the same journey of the Christian life with its adventures and battles, going into the unknown ahead of me. I can still see the painted pictures as they advanced with the story around the walls of the assembly hall.

Many of our teachers were brave single women. All had come out as missionaries and accepted the calling of teaching us so that our parents could fulfill their calling to preach the Gospel in China. Quite a few had been children of CIM missionaries and had attended Chefoo School themselves. Their parents had been pioneers and, true to the spirit of the Mission, had sent their children off, covering their real feelings and bearing it all bravely in the true British spirit. These teachers didn't give the impression of being sensitive to our struggle to cope with absence from parents. They had gone through it and had survived. The true-blue British stiff-upper-lip approach tended to come through. For any of us the luxury of a good cry was discouraged as far as I can remember.

There were two teachers in particular, however, whose love and gentleness touched me in a special way and helped to take my mother's place. Miss Young was like her name, Pearl; and Miss Getgood was likewise so. Their love showed, and we loved them in return.

Caring for us outside of class time were housekeepers and "wardrobe mistresses," as they were quaintly termed. They looked after us in all the daily detail of life at boarding school, from reading to us the letters from our parents to mending our clothes and fitting us into hand-me-downs. A number of the housekeepers had been widowed early in their missionary life through accident or sickness encountered in the remote areas where they worked. They

gladly became mothers to much larger families on moving to
Chefoo, and we as children responded to their affectionate
care. They filled our days with useful activities and our minds
with still-vibrant memories.

We learned how to knit, watching the teacher demonstrate
with rope and cricket stumps. Our class kept silkworms and
wound off the silk from the cocoons. Hopscotch, marbles, and
soccer were my favorite activities. On weekends we wore our
white uniforms, little shirts with shorts that buttoned on round
the waist. Early Sunday mornings we lined up in pairs and
wound our way out of the compound in a long line under the
interested gaze of the local people as we made our way to
church.

We walked along the seafront through the foreign settlement,
passing the Chefoo Club and homes of the Western business
community en route to the Union Church or the Anglican
Church. The Reverend Mr. Stocker in his robes stood before
the altar with his back towards us and raised his high-pitched
voice in supplication. There we stood in angelic awe, back in
the dark recesses, row upon row of silent or mumbling forms
as reverence was inculcated into our spirits.

In the afternoon we were out in our crocodile lines again on
our regular Sunday walks. The foreign cemetery was a favorite
destination. In keeping with the principles of the Sabbath, we
were not allowed to run around, but the upright gravestones
and monuments of some of the missionary pioneers served us
well for hide-and-seek at walking pace. I was hushed to a deep
pondering when I came face-to-face with the headstones of the
thirteen Chefoo boys who had died of ptomaine poisoning in
1904 when they had eaten chicken pies that had gone bad. The
cemetery had a kind of haunting appeal for me. Written large
on one of the graves were the words: "In such a time as ye

think not, the Son of Man cometh." *Would Jesus come back before I saw my parents again?* I wondered as we ambled back in column to school.

Sunday afternoon was also the time for writing letters home. One time at the cemetery I had a bright idea: *If I get a bee-sting on my hand, I won't be able to write, and I'll get out of letter-writing!* The hollyhocks along the paths were a favorite target of the bees. I took my chance at the end of the line on the way out of the cemetery to capture a bee inside the petals, and carried my prisoner back to school. While those around me were sucking their pencils or looking to the ceiling for inspiration, I was probing the depths of the hollyhock to apprehend the captive. Getting it between my fingers I pulled it out gingerly and began to squeeze and poke it provocatively with my right forefinger. It did everything but sting me! In exasperation I pushed it back into the petals, but as I did so, I absent-mindedly used my left hand, and in a flash the pain stabbed up my finger. It was my first lesson on nature's unintentioned irony. What good was a sting on my left hand as I am right-handed!

Some memories, however, are more pleasant. I remember the joys of the walks up into the hills to the Bamboo Temple, the Monastery, and Adam's Knob, and trips out to Bottle Rock, the Bluff, or Lighthouse Island with its beautiful white sand.

The games, sports and activities were unforgettable. We had a game called "Prisoner's Base," in which we tried to free those captured by the other side. Treasure hunts were really great fun—even the time I found the treasure, only to discover it was a necklace, and I had to give it to my sister!

In general we were one big, happy family and enjoyed our very special kind of life. In retrospect, however, experiences of pain and fear seem to have left the deepest impression among my recollections of the first two years at school. Some of the punishments were quite Victorian, and perhaps all the more effective for that. The lingering taste of Lifebuoy soap after we had our mouths washed out with a toothbrush made telling lies very unpopular.

An effective method for curbing bullies' aggression towards the girls was the "Punching Post," an unfriendly-looking concrete supporting pillar beside the playing quadrangle. Anyone caught fighting had to punch the stout post with his bare hands. If the offender didn't punch it hard enough, he was sometimes given assistance to give him bruised knuckles as a helpful reminder to take away with him. Thus were our gentlemanly manners refined and the fairer sex preserved from bruises.

That didn't makes us angels, however. For instance, on many a night after our dorm of eight seven-year-olds had been tucked into bed after evening prayers we would creep out from under the blankets. Using a book and a rolled-up sock, we would have a game of "dorm cricket" in the middle of the room —until we were caught.

At other times, master storyteller David Birch, whose younger brother John was in my dorm, would creep stealthily down from "Big End." He held us enthralled with his stories of trapdoors and long, dark tunnels with pirates and hidden treasure bulging from old oak chests. The stories were so good that I remember a time when we discovered some of the teachers listening behind the door.

It could have been these graphic late-night tales or fear of being kidnapped by the thieves who were caught sometimes climbing over the compound wall that gave us nightmares. Although it was a comfort to have the family picture hanging above my bed beside my school number, which was 66, I threaded my arm some nights under the mattress and between

The Michells leaving for furlough from Fengsiang, Shensi, in July 1937. From left to right on top of the baggage are David, his sisters Joyce and Joan, and his mother.

Travel by bus in inland China during the 1930s could be considerably more unpredictable than travel by horse-drawn conveyance. This bus in which the Michells traveled was all too typical of transportation available in those days.

The main building of the Prep School at Chefoo and the steps on which David Michell took his stand when he was six.

David's passport picture when he was eight.

Big sister Joyce Michell ready to try her hand at tennis during her Prep School days at Chefoo.

David Michell, John Taylor, and David Allen playing in the "Quadrangle" at the Prep School.

Weihsien guard towers from outside the walls.

The hospital at Weihsien. Chefoo kids used the attic of the hospital for classrooms.

Block 23 in Weihsien Concentration Camp. David Michell
and other younger children shared a room at the right end of
the building. Eric Liddell lived in the room directly above.

Weihsien

Kitchen Number One.

Constant reminder of the Japanese and imprisonment: the searchlight towers.

Weihsien Cub Scouts: The girls: Since the author knew the girls less well than he did the boys, forty years has made identification of the Brownies almost impossible.

Leaders: *(Middle row, center)* Norman Cliff, Evelyn Davey (Huebener), Isabel Harris.
Boys: *(Front row)* Philip Paulson, Paul Grant, Val Nicholls, David Michell, Ray Moore, John Taylor, Robert Clow, and John Birch (David Allen was absent).

Home on the *Gripsholm*

Part of the China Inland Mission group repatriated from Weihsien and Shanghai on the *Gripsholm* in late 1943. Here behind the Philadelphia headquarters are *(back row)* Mrs. H. E. V. Andrews, Rev. H. E. V. Andrews, Miss Martha Philips, Frederick Harris, Rev. Elden Whipple, (Rev. Herbert Griffin, Home Director); *(second row)* Bernice Kohfield, Fronsie Beckon, Miss Marjorie Simpson, Miss Laura Robinson, Miss Dorothea Foucar, Mary Pearl Nowack, Barbara Hulse, Kathryn Kuhn, Nathan Walton; *(third row)* Mrs. R. D. Thomas, David Thomas, Hugh Hulse, Elden Whipple, Jr., and Julia Whipple, Bruce Kohfield, Lorna Lee Whipple, Lois (Lindie) Walton (today the wife of the U.S. Director) and Barbara Walton; *(front row)* Byron Kohfield, Kathleen Smail, Nathan Thomas Walton, Ian Smail, and Dwight Whipple.

Photograph by the Philadelphia *Evening Bulletin*.

Eric Liddell

Eric Liddell at the 1924 British Empire Games. It was that same year at the Olympic Games that he won the Gold Medal in the 400-meter race after refusing to run in his best event, the 100-meter race, because it was scheduled to be run on Sunday.

Gene Heubener reading in the room that he shared with Eric Liddell and others in internment camp at Weihsien during the days Eric was helping with recreation in camp, including that of Chefoo schoolchildren.

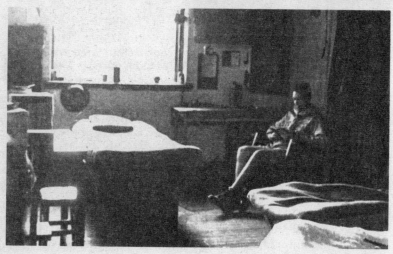

Weihsien's wall, guard tower, and the hospital where Eric Liddell died of a brain tumor only months before liberation.

The wooden cross marking Eric's grave in the Japanese quarter of the Weihsien compound.

Following the arrival at Weihsien of the seven U.S. airmen in August 1945, B29s dropping supplies by parachute beyond the bell tower of Block 23, by this time flying the American flag.

Hudson Taylor's son Herbert, 85 at liberation, not only survived internment camp, but lived five more years in England.

Liberation

Liberated Weihsien internees spill out of the train at Tsingtao. Center front is Pa Bruce.

Older Chefoo students celebrate their freedom on the beach at Tsingtao with Lt. James Moore (c.), former Chefusian who parachuted into Weihsien.

40 Years Later

潍 坊

WEIFANG

On August 17, 1985, arriving at the train station at today's Weihsien, now called Weifang: Ken Michell, David Michell, Mary Broughton, John Hoyte, James Broughton, Jonathan Hoyte, and Cyril Weller.

This plaque is presented by the CIM Chefoo Schools Association to Commemorate with deep gratitude

- The 40th anniversary of the liberation of 1400 prisoners, including about 500 children, from Weihsien Internment Camp by 7 American GIs on August 17, 1945, at the end of World War II.
- The last resting place of Eric Liddell, Olympic hero of "Chariots of Fire," who died in the camp February 21, 1945

Mary H. Broughton

John M. Hoyte

David J. Michell

August 17, 1985

内地会芜罘学校校友会怀着深厚的感激之情恭献
这面横额以纪念

＊1945年8月17日第二次世界大战结束时七位
美军士兵解放潍县拘留营1400名囚犯（包
括约500名儿童）四十周年

＊奥林匹克运动会 "火车""Chariots of Fire,"
英雄埃里克·利德尔（1945年2月21日逝世
于拘留营）安息之处

玛丽·H·布罗顿
约翰·M·霍伊特
大卫·J·米歇尔

1985年8月17日

The plaque that now hangs at the site of Weihsien Camp.

Not being strangers to chopsticks,
the three teenagers in the party—Ken Michell,
Jonathan Hoyte, and James Broughton—
enjoy a bowl of noodles on the street,
the local equivalent to fast foods.

Block 23 as the author and fellow visitors found it in 1985, part of the bell tower missing, but quite recognizable. The younger Chefoo boys lived in a room at the far right.

Below: Before presenting the plaque to be displayed as a historical marker at the one-time prison camp, the returnees pose with officials of the school now occupying the site.

Chefoo/Weihsien Internment Camp reunion in Toronto in 1982 includes Eric Liddell's widow. *Front row:* Roy Seaman, Gordon Martin, Mrs. Florence Liddell Hall, and Mrs. C. B. Hanna. *Middle row:* Agnes (Bell) Roswell, Irene Rouse, Doris and Grace Seaman, Marjory Windsor, Roxie (Hanna) Wilson, and Dr. James H. Taylor III. *Back row:* David Michell, Isabel Taylor, and Mrs. Grace (Taylor) Harris.

the steel springs, so that no one would be able to carry me away without my waking.

Richard Tennant (not his real name) slept in the bed next to mine. Our regular pre-supper ritual was a quick rinse in the washbowls of warm water poured out ahead of time for us. One evening, coming in late, Tennant rushed into the washroom and thrust his hands into the bowl without looking. He let out a yell of pain as he put his hands on a scorpion. Perhaps it was a lesson for all of us to be a little more careful. I think it was a few nights later that poor Tennant had trouble again.

We were all in bed in the dorm, and our clandestine storyteller had sneaked back quietly to his room. Some gentle snores were coming from the beds further away, but right beside me, whimpers emanated from a heaving mound under the covers.

Lifting my head very timidly, I peered above the sheets and found my dormmates doing likewise. We were staring at the moaning heap at the foot of Tennant's bed. Soon the moans turned to groans, then loud cries as he sobbed for his mother. We could see his bed shaking. This went on for quite a while until in a yelling crescendo, Tennant flew up into the air, blankets flying above him, and then crashed down in a crumpled heap onto the bed once more. His nightmare over, the room grew quiet again, and we burrowed deeper beneath our covers, shaking, to try to sleep. None of us spoke, and we all felt very scared and alone. We had never seen anything like this before. How could he jump that high in his sleep? The event took on an almost supernatural aura in our minds as we compared notes the next morning. As we exchanged impressions, our estimates of the height of Tennant's midnight leap ranged from a foot above the bed, to hitting the ceiling. Perhaps such daily trivia kept us from undue preoccupation with the national events sweeping our land.

Although war clouds were growing ever darker around us, the teachers spared us from the anxieties and fears that they must have felt. The motto of the Mission's founder—"Hold God's faithfulness" (paraphrase of "Have faith in God")—stood us all in good stead.

As early in the Japan-China conflict as October 1940, Pat A. Bruce, the school's headmaster, known as "Pa Bruce," wrote the following letter to all parents:

> You are sure to have heard of the advice given by the American consular authorities to their nationals to leave China as soon as possible. British authorities have not sent out any such advice, though it is evident to us that the situation is serious. We in Council have spent many hours discussing the situation in its various aspects, particularly in relation to the Chefoo Schools.
>
> Our General Director, Bishop Houghton, and I went to interview the highest available British Embassy official, and after that, with Mr. Dreyer, went to see an important American consular officer.
>
> Both these authorities concur with our opinion that, in spite of the threatening outlook, our only course of action is to continue to keep the schools open. In any provision for the care of the children, the British authorities have agreed to treat the Schools as a unit, without discrimination of nationality.
>
> This decision to keep the schools open in Chefoo has only been arrived at after fully facing the possibilities that might arise in the event of conflict in the Far East, because we realize the impossibility of moving as a unit to any one of the home countries. The Chefoo Schools have weathered many a storm in the last sixty years, undoubtedly owing to the prayers of parents and scores of others interested the world over, and I believe that this will be the case again. Anyhow, nothing can touch us apart from the permissive will of God, who undoubtedly causes all things to work together for good to those that love Him. This is the fact upon which we now rely.
>
> I understand that a cable is being sent to the home centers telling of this decision to remain open and asking for special prayer for the schools during these critical days.
>
> Yours very sincerely, Pat A. Bruce

The schools did stay open, but travel for a number of us was either too dangerous or not permitted by the authorities. This meant we could not see our parents, even at Christmas, but the school staff did all they could to make Christmas a happy time for us. Extracts from another letter to the parents and kept by my Mum and Dad all these years tell about the exciting times we had:

China Inland Mission
Prep School Chefoo
27th December, 1940

Dear Parents of Prepites:

Christmas Day 1940 has just passed, and we who have spent it with your children want to tell you, who must have longed to do so, something of the happenings.

We began the holidays with about fifty Prepites, and, perhaps because we were such a large family, the spirit of Christmas came to us very early.

. . . Just before Christmas the well-known story of Scrooge once again delighted youthful eyes and ears and prepared the way for the Spirit of Christmas 1940. On Christmas Eve little messengers went round the compound or to the houses of other friends carrying bulging bags, waste paper [baskets], or even laundry baskets full of gifts, while others with dolls' prams filled them with gay packages and wheeled them off. Meanwhile a bevy of artists from the Girls' House transformed our dining room into a Christmas bower, where red and green and silver glowed in the soft lights from the tree.

Just as supper was over a Chinese school visited us and filled the hall with their hearty singing while our children looked on in solemn amazement. Then, as the last of our excited little family jumped into bed, the corridors were lit by torches, and another bank of carollers gave us the sweet, familiar music that rings in Christmas for us Westerners whether at home or abroad. These were rewarded by [our] donations to a box marked "Relief" which, at the end of the evening held nearly $200.

That night a package found its way on to the foot of each bed, not quite burning a hole through the covers in the few short hours till

Christmas Day in the morning. That morning began at 6:30, and instead of the clanging of a gong, church bells relayed by a gramophone echoed down the passages. Breakfast was followed by family prayers round the table, and again the soft lights on the tree shed their radiance over a scene which you would love to have looked upon. Our hearts bowed in worship as we sang of the One who came, "A little Child to earth, long ago" from the knowledge of whom comes all peace and joy and love.

After a short interval we met again in families to open the presents which lay stacked up on floor or tables, and I wish you could have seen how eyes sparkled as books, dolls, aeroplanes, torches [flashlights], penknives or a photograph of you, emerged from their wrappings.

. . . Real families with members in any of the schools, sat together for the service . . . Mr. Clarence Preedy led the service in a Memorial Hall beautifully decorated for the occasion. On the platform was a small Christmas tree with real parcels at its base. These Mr. Preedy opened one by one revealing lettering that reminded us of some of God's gifts to us; beginning, of course, with the Gift of His Son. Dinner of goose, plum pudding, mince pies and all the appropriate accompaniments thereof, was served to nearly 150 people in the Prep diningroom. . . . Each diner was provided with a paper hat, and soon the scene was gay and animated indeed. . . . Mr. Bruce . . . voiced our thanks to all who had helped to prepare the meal, and to the friend in England who had given so generously towards it.

At 5:00 p.m. we all made our way to the Memorial Hall for the final thrill of the day. The platform had been transformed into a well. A curtain mysteriously draped one stairway leading to it, while the center was lit by fairy lights. At once the whisper went round, "Father Christmas (Santa Claus) is going to come out of the well." At length . . . Father Christmas himself appeared, a dignified figure in spite of his somewhat small and unsteady conveyance. Once on the platform, he found no difficulty in making the well produce suitable gifts for all. At last came the gifts for all the girls and boys; a well-filled stocking for those of Prepite age and something more useful or enduring for those of riper years. His work well and nobly done, Father Christmas was wheeled out of the Hall followed by admiring and affectionate glances, and tired but contented little people made their way home to supper and bed.

. . . Let us together thank the Great Giver of every good and perfect gift, whose loving-kindness alone made such a world at such a time as this.

Such a Christmas in such a world and at such a time had both a present as well as a prophetic message as the years ahead were to disclose. Humanly speaking, there could have been feelings of loneliness and uncertainty, but none of us ever heard or saw any reason to doubt that our Christmas experience was one of Emmanuel—God with us.

With the advent of 1941, changes in China began to accelerate. Missionaries' and business people's movements became more restricted. Few new pupils could come to the Chefoo Schools. That year the pupils numbered only 327, and that included a number of day-students from the Chefoo foreign business community.

We had grown accustomed to the presence of the Japanese armies in the region. They had mustered a large army of puppet soldiers out of disgruntled local citizenry who swallowed their propaganda. Freedom for commerce and travel for the Chinese was severely curtailed, and Japanese language took the place of English in the Chinese schools' curriculum. Skirmishes between the Japanese and their puppet army against the communists and the guerrilla forces loyal to the Nationalists were increasing all the time. Soldiers began to include our compound and activities in their investigations.

One day Gordon Martin, the Latin teacher, affectionately known as "Goopy," saw some figures in military uniform crossing the playground as he taught his class. "Our new rulers have arrived," he remarked calmly. We sensed the war was coming closer to us but little realized how close. Prayer took on a more urgent note.

Japan had promised China freedom from Western Imperialism. Her entry into China had been in the interests of consolidating the "Greater East Asia Co-Prosperity Sphere," which was to stretch from Burma and Sumatra to Manchuria. The early enthusiasm in the north of China by those who saw Japan as a savior from domination by the West soon turned to disillusionment and bitter hatred. Japan felt driven to even more aggressive alternatives when the United States, with the support of Holland and Britain, cut off oil shipments to Japan. The militarists in the government who had been responsible four years earlier for Japan's invasion into China prevailed in their determination to expand the war. The result has gone down in history—the attack on the U.S. Pacific Fleet at Pearl Harbor on Sunday, December 7, 1941.

Life for us was about to change—drastically.

Chapter 4

BAYONETS IN
THE SCHOOL YARD

"All that travel by land or by water,
all women laboring of child, all sick persons,
and young children; and to shew thy pity
upon all prisoners and captives."

—The Litany, *The Book of Common prayer*.

W e first heard news of the Pearl Harbor
attack the following morning when some
of the boys returned for school after
spending the weekend with the McMullans,
one of the nearby business families. The reports were confirmed not only from the radio, but by the hail of stones over
our wall from boys at the Japanese School that had been built
adjacent to us.

Goopy Martin was on duty at the Boys' School that morning
when a military truck arrived at the main gate and the soldiers
and their retinue demanded to see the principal, Pat Bruce.
Helplessly he led them into the school. Pa Bruce had traveled

back via Siberia from his last furlough, and this put him under suspicion of spying. Along with five Western businessmen, who symbolized colonial financial interests, Pa Bruce was trundled off to imprisonment at the Astor House Hotel on the Bund. Rigorous interrogation followed, and the men were locked up in separate rooms. Back at school all of us were praying.

But there was no immediate release. Day after day the prayers of students and teachers alike pleaded with God for His protection and Pa Bruce's release. To the delight of all, the men were given a day-pass to be home for Christmas. But by 9:00 the next morning all were back under lock and key.

When a whole month later Pa Bruce was released, we welcomed our much thinner and worn-looking principal back with great relief and gratitude. Four of the businessmen who were interned with him—including Arthur Rouse, who did so much for us at the school—were freed too. But Bobs McMullan, the one still held in captivity, died some months later, though the family had been promised his release. He died of typhus and is buried in Chefoo.

There was no hiding the interest of the Japanese soldiers in our school property. No sooner had they taken over than they nailed a notice onto the wall beside the gate, stating that the compound was now the property of His Imperial Majesty, the Emperor of Japan. Soldiers marched in and took possession of radios and helped themselves to food in the kitchens and homes. They required detailed lists of all school and personal property, including furnishings, fittings, crockery, cutlery, etc.

For the time being, however, we managed to carry on with our school lessons almost normally. Following the formal declaration of war against Japan by the Western powers, we were all issued arm bands. Each of us had a number and identification of nationality—A for American, B for British, N for Norwegian, and X for any other "enemy nationals." We had to wear these to be allowed out of our school compound for walks.

As the weeks progressed in 1942, conditions deteriorated. News from China's far southwest was that I had a baby brother—Brian. But when, I fretted, would I ever see him?

Official Japanese visits to the school were becoming more frequent. When the respect did not come up to the military officers' expectation, they bellowed orders and reprimands. Gordon Martin recalls one high-ranking officer's haranguing the staff about the greatness of the Emperor and the might of the Japanese nation. He held up an enamel soap-dish which happened to be on the table in the staff room and shouted, "Even this dish belongs to the Emperor." Horse stables were erected behind the Business Department. Bayonet practice with blood-curdling shouts of *Yaa!* formed part of our daily entertainment. We grew accustomed to the sight of soldiers straggling in bleeding and wounded from battles in the hills. Although we were sheltered from seeing the sufferings of the local Chinese people, we heard about atrocities and sometimes heard and saw the results of beatings.

The current situation, like the arrest of our headmaster earlier, was greeted with solemn faces and a good deal of prayer. But there was no hint of panic. Never do I remember a note of alarm, fear or confusion in it all. It was simply something that happened and over which God had control. A letter smuggled out to the parents of two Swiss children at Chefoo indicated how the school was carrying on in these more oppressive times. The parents sent the news on to the China Director:

Kaifeng
Feb. 9, 1942

Dear Mr. Sinton,

The following extract is from a personal letter just received from one of the staff at Chefoo, and knowing the difficulties of the times, I thought it good to send it on to you in case you might be feeling some anxiety about the children.

"It must be weeks since you heard of the children, for no mails are allowed in or out these days . . . .

"We have cut down our meat and milk bills by half and dismissed a number of servants. The boys and girls in the other schools set the tables and clean rooms. Here the staff do their chores and spread bread. It is quite a business to clean your room before school in the mornings. We are also limited in the number of pieces of bread that we eat; the Preps eat nine a day. At supper they are allowed one every five minutes, and each is very particular that no one gets over his share. We are having the most interesting meals, *tou-fu* (bean curd) in a large loaf for dinner.

"Of course we see no fruit, though we have a lot of vegetables and often have raw cabbage and carrots for a salad. I am sure that no one has talked so much about food for years. We spend absolutely no money outside the compound more than is absolutely necessary. We are ripping up war knitting, scarves, etc., and making them into cardigans for the children. The staff are busy knitting stockings and other necessities.

"I wish that I could tell you of the wonderful way that God led certain people to prepare for this contingency. Others outside the compound were fearful of changing money at a low exchange and were left with almost nil and a small stock of coal, whereas the head of affairs in the compound had laid in a stock of coal for the winter, and it was wonderfully sent in when there seemed none to be had. Also Mr. Jackson had been extraordinarily wise, you can guess along what line. Then at Christmas, our puddings had been made weeks beforehand when supplies were not short, and Mr. Oleson very nobly killed one of his goats to supply most of the compound with Christmas fare.

"Then as for presents! We could almost write a book on the way the Preps were able to have about five little parcels each. Just the day or so before things closed up a large parcel post came in from Shanghai bringing quite a store of children's presents from parents down there. An evacuating mother left a veritable toyshop behind with Miss Carr, and the toys were all as good as new. Two large parcels for a little boy in Kansu had been lying with us for a year or two, and we took the liberty of disposing of its contents. Another evacuating child left us with ten tins of jam. Another parcel from America with gifts of books came too late for last Christmas and came in handy this one. It was marvelous.

"Then we have been so glad to hold our Memorial Hall services, so that we could all meet together on Christmas morning. In the afternoon we had games as usual and then the Boys' School put on a very good puppet show, which was followed by Father Christmas coming down the chimney. He came with cholera certificates and the usual passes and enormous photos of himself. Mr. Bruce and most of the inmates of Astor House were allowed home for Christmas and had to report again next morning at 9:00 a.m."

I trust that this good news will bring some cheer to parents' hearts in inland stations. We here at Kaifeng are well and the Lord is wonderfully undertaking for us though the hospital is being run with our staff as a J. [Japanese] concern. They have supplied doctors and superintending nurses. We thank God that the chapel has not been interfered with and we have our regular services and the Lord has used this time of trial for the renewal and growth of the faith of many. Out of all the tribulations of these times He is gathering a people to His Name.

Yours in His service,
WINNIFRED C. URECH

The Japanese steadily encroached into more and more areas of the compound and our school life. Their baseball games often interfered with our cricket matches. They used the playing field for games on Sundays, and when our teachers lodged a written protest, it led to a severe rebuke from the military officers. In their tirade on "The Rights of Man," we discovered that nothing whatsoever belonged to us, and anything we did use was only by their sufferance.

After Pearl Harbor the efforts were redoubled to relocate the Schools to Free China or to some other country. Ernest Weller, one of the Mission leaders in Shanghai, cabled the Mission headquarters in Chungking (Chongqing) on April 16, 1942, the following message:

> Forced evacuation Chefoo probable, Swiss Consul appealing Tokio [Tokyo]. Transfer Shanghai or Free China impossible. South Africa in sterling block, central (to home countries). Trade Commissioner sailing end May, willing endeavor secure loan premises for duration (war) avoid scattering school.

What this all meant was that every effort was made to move to another country. South Africa or Lourenco Marques in Portuguese East Africa, the nearest neutral port, were rumored as our likely destination, but despite the work of Mr. Egger, the Swiss Consul in Tsingtao, nothing materialized. We heard later that the British Embassy felt it was not safe or practicable under such conditions to evacuate so large a number of children. Thus the cherished hopes of parents, teachers and children that we might get out of enemy-occupied territory came to nought.

That summer arrangements were made for a number of children whose parents were due for furlough or who worked in the northeast region to leave. Some other parents for various reasons postponed departure until the end of the year, little realizing what that few months' delay would mean. The Japanese moved in and occupied their region, closing it to all travel. They would not be free to leave again for almost four years.

If Victorian England had its Gilbert and Sullivan, Chefoo of the war years had its Martin and Houghton. All through the war years, for instance, we sang Psalm 46, put to music by Stanley Houghton, and through singing it in times of stress, the Psalm came alive to us. Stanley Houghton explains his writing of the chorus:

> At the beginning of the Summer Term, 1942, the Headmaster of the Chefoo Schools, Mr. P. A. Bruce, conducted the school service. He took for his text the opening verses of Ps. 46 and the refrain, "The Lord of Hosts is with us; the God of Jacob is our refuge." Never had the meaning come home to me with such power, in view of the presence of the Japanese and the uncertainty of the future. I wrote this chorus almost immediately as the expression of my deep feeling . . . ."[1]

Darkening shadows of the inevitable were closing in as more soldiers were posted to guard the school and we were prohibited from leaving the compound. With the lighter food rations more children were losing weight, but hearty doses of cod-liver oil prevented serious malnutrition.

The spring holidays that April were memorable for the evangelistic mission that was held on the beach and the east quadrangle by the Prep School. Arthur Rouse, one of the businessmen who lived near the school, his brother Albert, and a number of others including David Bentley-Taylor led special meetings under the auspices of the Children's Special Service Mission (CSSM). David Bentley-Taylor had a very dramatic way of making Bible stories come alive and the truth come home personally.

David had been one of the new missionary recruits who came to China in 1938 and who had been posted to Chefoo in 1939 for their initial missionary training—the group affectionately dubbed "The Sons of the Prophets." David had stayed on to join the Chefoo staff when conditions in China precluded his

[1]George A. Scott, *In Whose Hands? A Story of Internment in China* (London: China Inland Mission, n.d.), p. 33.

working elsewhere. He was the uncle of Raymond Moore, one of the boys in my class. I really liked David Bentley-Taylor's stories, but I remember resenting the fact that one of the boys in my class had a real uncle so near when the rest of us had no one from our families!

I enjoyed the choruses we sang during the mission, one of which spoke to my heart of what Jesus had done for me. In simple, childlike faith I sang it and meant it as I chose the way of Jesus for my life:

> All the way to Calvary
> He went for me, He went for me.
> All the way to Calvary
> He went for me,
> And that's the way for me.

With the Japanese soldiers roaming all around our compound, we no longer had exclusive right to buildings and playing fields to organize events. The soldiers took over the boys' field and showed propaganda films to several hundred Chinese brought in unwillingly.

Each year Chefoo School Foundation Day, June 15, was a special occasion. Despite wartime conditions, the 1942 celebration was as happy as ever. But there was one problem. The Japanese had taken the boats. We sadly missed the boat races when the two crews, Hero and Leander, vied annually against each other. The thirty boys and girls who would have formed the Boat Clubs had a picnic instead, in the gully running through the property. School boating songs followed the fun and games. Then the boys headed for the beach for a swim and ducked each other by the light of the moon. We Prep School boys, being but first and second graders, could enjoy all this only from our dorm window. How we longed for the day to come when we could be in the Boys' School and do such grown-up things!

The cricket match was, as always, the highlight of the day. As usual, the staff played the boys. Despite the age differences, the staff held their own and came out victorious, as we knew they would. Somehow it seemed a fitting end for what was destined to be the last in the long history of Foundation Day competitions.

Tennis matches, our Foundation Day Service, and an evening concert in the Memorial Hall completed a full and happy day. Gordon Welch, one of the staff, spoke on the foundation of God with its double seal, "Nevertheless, God's solid foundation stands firm, sealed with this inscription: 'The Lord knows those who are his,' and 'Everyone who confesses the name of the Lord must turn away from wickedness'" (2 Timothy 2:19). In the days ahead, though stone and concrete foundations had to be left behind, the living foundation of the School—God's promises and presence—continued with us.

In one of the last letters slipped out before our internment, one of the teachers penned in her diary:

> If the whole saga of these months could be written, it would make a splendid story with the children coming up trumps—hardly a Chefoo expression! Several boys who had been prayed for over a long time accepted Christ as their Savior. We are full of praise for all that God has done, is doing, and is going to do in the coming days.

The boat races, cricket matches, and Sports Days were all spoken of as likely to be our last. In the Prep School we all wondered who would have the honor of the last birthday before evacuation. As it turned out, I did.

I remember the celebration well. At the Child's Last Supper, as it were, I had my special friends, according to the time-honored rite, seated with me around one of the long tables set apart from the others in the Dining Hall. We feasted on the stack of peanut-buttered slices of bread made by the school's expert Chinese cook. In no time these and the Chinese treacle sandwiches alongside were demolished.

It was always a race to try to get the top slice of the peanut butter, known as "peries," or the bottom treacle-soaked slice, known as "scrape." The top piece always had the peanut butter piled up high and often carried the bonus of more adhering to the underside from the slice below. What delicious midnight feasts rolled-up peanut-butter balls made in the safety of the dorm!

*T*ime was indeed running out for us at Chefoo. In August the Japanese took over the hospital, the doctor's house, and staff block. Then in mid-October the soldiers marched in, demanding we vacate the Prep School building as this was the newest of the buildings, and the army wanted it. We were given a few days to move, boys in with the bigger boys in the Boys' School and the girls doubling up with the bigger girls in the Girls' School. In both cases, moving two full schools into one, made conditions very crowded. Classrooms had to be sacrificed for sleeping areas.

Girls' School building from 1896 to 1942.   *Drawings by Helen Fox.*

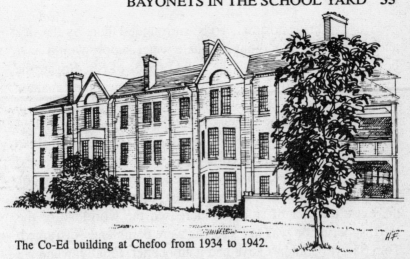

The Co-Ed building at Chefoo from 1934 to 1942.

Just before we moved, Miss Beatrice Stark, my teacher in Transition (Grade 2), found one of the Japanese officers sitting in the armchair in her room. His gaze was fixed on the large painting of the Good Shepherd. She told him to take it when we were gone, and her last act before leaving was to kneel down and pray for this major and the soldier who would occupy her room. On the last Sunday before departure for internment she heard the tune of "Jesus Loves Me" being picked out on the piano in the Memorial Hall. On peeking in, she found it was this same major. Had he come in contact with the Gospel somewhere?

One by one during the next three weeks or so the Japanese requisitioned the other buildings on the compound, and finally orders came that we had five days to be gone for good. Five days to move a school of two hundred children plus teachers and staff under wartime conditions. Where could we go?

The Japanese were "suggesting" the Cathay Hotel, a summer residence not far away on the East Beach. Cathay Hotel sounded nice enough, but it was dirty and run-down and was being

used as a military hospital. To be surrounded there by the sick
and wounded and without adequate water supply would have
been chaotic. But through the good offices of Mr. Egger, the
Swiss Consul, and the International Red Cross, the Japanese
scrapped this plan. We saw God's good hand caring for us in
this. Instead, we were told we would be moving into buildings
of the American Presbyterian Mission at Temple Hill, about
two miles inland from our compound.

After our transfer from the Prep School to the Boys' School,
we younger children were having a real-life adventure. Because
the extra number of students increased the workload of the
staff, supervision was lax. Classes were completely disrupted.
Tom Sawyer couldn't have had it any better. Finally, when we
prepared to leave, the dream of every schoolboy was fulfilled
when the teachers told us we could take anything we wanted
from the staff room. How well I remember stuffing my pockets
from the teachers' desks with the confiscated treasures of by-
gone years. Bunches of old keys, coins, marbles, light bulbs,
spools, and junk of all descriptions bulged from our pockets as
we rattled upstairs to our makeshift beds in the dormitories.

The day of departure the teachers commanded
each of us to take our bedside potties with us.
Many a time in the coming months these enamel or
china potties were the subject of self-congratulation on the part
of the teachers, but for us they were a constant source of em-
barrassment. I was glad I had an enamel one, as the huge china
ones brought mortifying blushes to the poor souls who had to
bear these undisguisable burdens! Nevertheless, my personal
potty kept me company until the war was over.

Early the next morning we were herded together outside. It
was the 5th of November, 1942. The very youngest were put

in rickshaws with their cabin trunks. The older CIMers who had retired at Chefoo were also allowed to ride. The rest of us loaded our stuff onto an old truck and prepared to walk the two miles or so to our next "home." We were lined up in twos, with the guards alongside shouting orders.

What an emotional time it was for ones like Mrs. Emily Clinton, who had spent more than thirty years as housekeeper in the Prep, Girls', and Boys' Schools! Likewise for Mr. and Mrs. William Taylor, two of the earliest missionaries to join the CIM from North America back in the late 1880s. Then there was also Mr. Herbert Taylor at 82, Hudson Taylor's eldest son, who in the year of the founding of Chefoo School, over sixty years before, had cut short his studies at Cambridge to join his father in the work in China.

While the Japanese soldiers shouted orders outside, pushing and shoving everyone into line, some of the staff lingered for some final moments in the Prayer Room, before the simple inscription on the foundation-stone—"To the Glory of God, 1896." They paused in prayer and carried the glory with them as they walked out and joined the motley retinue lining up.

I stood with the other boys in my class. My hand felt in my little bundle of possessions for the one thing I couldn't bear to leave–my box of dominoes. They were still all there. Their carefully carved surface and smooth finish reassured me. My parents had chosen them especially for me. They were beautiful, and they were more precious now than ever—my one lifeline to family. I straightened my shoulders and moved smartly into line.

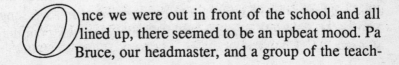

nce we were out in front of the school and all lined up, there seemed to be an upbeat mood. Pa Bruce, our headmaster, and a group of the teachers were standing outside the buildings as we began to file out towards the gate. Some threw longing glances backward: others struggled with the spirit of "going down with the ship" as it were, but they knew that all of us, their charges, were worth more than the buildings and the compound, despite the memories that flooded over them and appealed to hold them back.

Amid the shouts and yelling of the guards, some of the girls particularly were frightened and hugged their dolls. Miss Davey took the lead of the youngest group, who were eight- and nine-year-olds, and comforted them. As she strode forward ahead of her girls, the basket slung over her arm moved slightly and a tiny paw protruded. Quickly she pushed it back in and winked at the girls around her. The word was whispered around quickly, "Miss Davey smuggled out her cat!" The girls were delighted, the guards none the wiser.

As the school began to march out past the guards and mounted troops, we burst into singing:

> God is still on the throne
> And He will remember his own.
> Though burdens may press us
> And trials distress us,
> He never will leave us alone.
>
> God is still on the throne,
> And He will remember his own.
> His promise is true;
> He will not forget you.
> God is still on the throne.

Our long procession wound its way slowly to Temple Hill, the site of our first prison camp; crowds of Chinese lined the road, sadness on their faces. On the upward climb we sang Stanley Houghton's arrangement of Psalm 46, now so familiar to us:

The Lord is Our Refuge

Psalm 46:1–7

Stanley Houghton

God is our Ref-uge, our Re-fuge and our Strength in trou-ble, in

trou-ble a ver-y pres-ent help; There-fore will not we fear—

fear, will not we

There-fore will not we fear. The Lord of Hosts is with us, The

fear will not we fear, not fear.

Lord of Hosts is with us, The God of Ja-cob is our Ref - uge!

God is our Refuge,
Our Refuge and our Strength,
In trouble, in trouble,
A very present help.
Therefore will not we fear:
The Lord of Hosts is with us;
The God of Jacob is our Refuge.

One of the older boys in poignant parody describes his experiences in parting from the old school:

HIAWATHA LEAVES
FOR CONCENTRATION

By the shore of the Pacific,
By the shining big sea water,
At the gate of the big Compound,
On a pleasant Autumn morning
Hiawatha stood and waited.

All his bedding and his suitcase
Were now waiting to be taken;
Something in the hazy distance,
Something in the mists of morning
Coming nearer, nearer, nearer,
Came a lorry empty, rumbling,
Rattling as it came up nearer,
Came to take his pile of bedding,
Came to take his waiting suitcase,
Then to a meal went Hiawatha.

Seated at the central table,
Sprang he out from amongst his fellows,
Seized upon the choicest portions,
Seized the white fat from the hot stew
Set apart for prefect lofty.
Then the Matron softly whispered,
Whispered saying, "They are famished—
Let them do what best delights them;
Let them eat, for they are famished."

And the boys made answer saying,
"We have listened to your message;
We have heard your words of wisdom;
We will now eat on in silence."

Having fed with saddened visage,
From his place rose Hiawatha,
Bade farewell to the ancient boys' school,
Spake in a loud voice, spake in this wise,
"I am going, Oh, my old school, on a short
Yet distant journey.
Many moons will have come and vanished
E'er I come again to see you.
Our little friends will now possess you.
They may change and perhaps wreck you,
But I hope to be returning
From the land of Hill and Temple."

On the road stood Hiawatha,
Turned and waved his hand at parting,
On the clear and open big road
Launched his push bike into the roadway,
Whispered to it, "Westward, Westward"
And with speed it darted forward.
Thus departed Hiawatha;
Thus departed all the compound,
In the golden sun of autumn
To the regions of the temple,
To the land of concentration.

—Robin Hoyte

Chapter 5

INTERNMENT AT TEMPLE HILL

"By the waters of Babylon, there we sat down
and wept, when we remembered Zion."

—Psalm 137:1

Weary from our long march up the hill from our school at the coast, we were startled when seventy-one of our members, comprising the Girls' School mainly, were suddenly diverted to a six-room house in a compound a half mile off to the right. I got the last fleeting glimpse for many weeks of my sister as the long file, bowed down by their bedding bundles, disappeared down a dingy laneway. The rest of us straggled on to the left and eventually through a gateway with high walls stretching away on both sides.

This first internment camp was a Presbyterian Mission Compound. The part I was assigned to had three good-sized foreign-style homes with about eight rooms each. Our teachers got the message in a hurry that all 175 of our group had to be divided up into these three houses. We of the Prep School with our all-lady staff, plus eight older boys to do the heavy lifting, were put together with the Harrises and the Bazires, two of the Chefoo staff families. In all, seventy-two individuals took shelter in the home where the Burst family, former Presbyterian missionaries, once lived—and burst we nearly did!

In the next house were most of the Boys' School and their staff, a total of fifty-eight souls, and bulky bodies too, they discovered. The third house took our older missionaries who had retired in China and another eight boys to help with the work. They were positively rattling around with only forty-five to occupy their eight rooms.

Getting settled in was helped greatly by the Japanese having allowed the Martins and Mrs. Lack and her boys to go ahead to the camp the day before. Some of the luggage was brought out by truck and dumped outside the building.

To make sure nothing was stolen—as the houses had been looted already of their contents—Gordon Martin slept on the baggage pile that night. About midnight he heard what he thought was the sound of heavy drops of rain and woke with a start. To his great surprise, he discovered it wasn't rain, but the flock of goats that the advance party had brought over with them. The goats had broken out of their enclosure and, as is the habit of goats, were about to nibble at the precious baggage[1].

Truck loads of boxes arrived in the morning, and by the time we marched in, the advance party had been able to survive the smoke from an obstreperous wood stove and get a hot meal ready. It might have been goat stew had Mr. Martin not taken pity on the night marauders! Mercifully, three of the buildings had attics. That night scores of bright-eyed campers peeped out

[1] Gordon Martin, unpublished manuscript, *Memoirs* (Elmwood, Ontario, n.d.), p. 56.

from a patchwork quilt of bedding under the rafters, a rewarding sight for the tired teachers.

On our first day at the Temple Hill compound, Miss Davey wrote in her diary: "We had a picnic lunch on the steps in the midst of all the baggage. Gradually . . . rooms were swept and washed, Prepites' beds laid out on the floor, and the staff assigned to rooms in the Chinese servants' quarters. It was all friendly and picnic-like, and only the presence of the Japanese soldiers, complete with bayonets, reminded us that we really were being interned in enemy territory."

The picnic spirit continued for the first few days. We ate supper that first night on cabin trunks, sitting in our housecoats and pajamas.

For the teachers, used to having the cooking and many of the daily chores done by Chinese servants, life was extremely busy. Ben Hayman in my class prayed that night, "O Lord, bless the people in the kitchen who are working so hard, and help them to work harder and harder and harder"!

Next morning there was time to explore our new surroundings. Over the back wall and up the hill a little further, silhouetted against the sky line, was the temple which gave the area its name. It was the beautiful old Temple of Yu Hwang, the Jade Emperor. A six-hundred-year-old pomegranate tree in the inner courtyard gave eloquent witness to the antiquity of the sacred site. The Chefoo Convention of 1876, whereby China agreed to grant access to more ports for foreign trade, had been signed in these very temple precincts.

In the compound behind the three main houses were a number of smaller places: servants' quarters, a woodshed, laundry, and garage. These we searched with much excitement and found a good supply of old stamps which we treasured until the older boys, knowing their value better than we did, bullied them from us. All these cubbyholes were soon graded as the better-class private accommodations.

By far the biggest shock of the Temple Hill compound was the state of the outside toilets. I remember the first time necessity took a group of us to that region, which was near the back wall beyond the overgrown garden beds. The toilets lay flush to the ground in full public view, with no doors and only a tiled awning above. The pungent smell would have been enough to signal revulsion, but we pressed forward, jumping on the stones as we neared the target. I took one last long jump to find myself marooned on a stepping-stone island, surrounded by a seething sea of maggots. The memory is with me still.

Needless to say, with no more servants around, we all had to pitch in with much improvisation called for to meet our needs. Water was very scarce and had to be carried, with hot water being taken one way and cold water brought from the other direction. A lot of cleaning up had to be done as well. And we had to buy our

The Temple of Yu Hwang, from which Temple Hill got its name.

Drawing by Helen Fox.

own food, as the Japanese initially accepted no responsibility for this, although, later on, they sent in limited daily rations.

Even the coal supply we had was taken for "military purposes." However, some stoves were found, and each house had at least one fitted up. Many a time we were down to the last bucket of coal, but there was always enough to keep one room warm. Coal dust and clay mixed into coal balls saw us through the winter, but we often suffered the misery of chilblains and chapped hands and legs.

Everyone of us in camp had our regular chores, from sweeping floors to peeling potatoes. Literally jammed in between all this we pursued our lessons on trunks and boxes round the walls of our all-in-one classroom-living-room-dining-room-bedroom.

Getting washed at night—with 72 of us crowded into the one building and with such limited water—was a problem. Each of us would wash in his own little bit of water in his personal basin and then all of us would rinse in a common tub. Sometimes it happened that some culprit did such a poor job of washing himself that the rinse water became unusable!

Our teachers were ever resourceful in many areas as they carried on teaching us in these conditions. No less enterprising in supplying us with food, Mrs. Martin and Mrs. Lack branched out into mixed farming on a small scale to augment our limited food supply.

The latter two ladies bought two little pigs, each about twenty-five pounds in weight. "Rudolph" could scream like a two-hundred pounder, though his brother "Adolph" was more amenable. Fed on what scraps there were, the pigs grew quite rapidly, and we all looked forward with much anticipation to pork for Christmas dinner, instead of murky-looking liver or other mysterious parts of unknown animals. Wails of grief were heard to ascend just two days before Christmas when our budding farmers announced that "Rudolph" was gravely ill. The earnest prayer of many hungry children, combined with a dose of brandy and castor oil, did wonders, and our porcine friend, from our point of view, came to a happy end! The two pigs between them graced our humble table with about one hundred and sixty pounds of meat.

Chickens and geese were also added to the farmyard, but the geese had a nasty habit of nipping the girls' legs and met their Waterloo after taking on one of the lady teachers. The chickens, too, came to an untimely end when the basement flooded and drowned them.

Extras often came to us over the wall. Being German (a member of the Liebenzell Mission, an associate mission of the CIM), Rudolf Arendt was not interned. He and his family found ways of getting both food and mail to us, more than once dumping bags of rice over the wall at night. Young Sammy (now in Montreal) even managed to rescue Gordon Welch's goat from the Welch house, leading it through the streets of Chefoo and eventually into camp. Though not much relished by us children, goat's milk became a prime source of needed nourishment.

*I*n our struggle to cope with the cramped conditions and eking out our daily existence, many things played their part in keeping up our morale. Over in the Girls' School Camp, known as "Irwin House," they were likewise doing their best to make the most of their situation. Our principal was given permission to make periodic visits under escort and talk with the other staff members. Later on, all of us who had a sister in the other camp were allowed weekly visits. How we cherished these opportunities to breathe

the heady air of freedom and have brief contact as a family!

Morning prayers and camp services assumed increasing importance in our lives. In so many remarkable ways God supplied our needs. Sometimes Chinese friends passed money secretly over the wall to us by night. Later our need for outside cash diminished when the Japanese agreed with the Swiss Consul's demand that a cash grant of so much per day per person be given. We managed very well, considering the lot of so many of the Chinese people who were bordering on starvation, their bodies not much more than skin and bone.

Thieves, who climbed over the wall into camp, became a real problem. In her diary Evelyn Davey recorded:

> Lately we have had an epidemic of thieves. Pearl Young's trunk on the veranda was robbed one night. Another night Ettie Henderson's week's washing went from her veranda. A third night the ladies downstairs went out in their night attire, armed with dress-hangers to scare a thief away. And yet another night Mr. Bazire chased two men down the front drive with a poker! I have moved my trunks from the entrance and am sleeping on top of them. It's even harder than the floor.

The Temple Hill Tattler, our camp paper, made its appearance early in camp life. *The Tattler* gave us cleverly disguised news and also served to recount the humor of the evening concerts put on for us regularly by staff members and older students.

What a lift these concerts gave our spirits from the drudgery of the long months of internment! Featuring in one of the songs was Mr. Egger of the Swiss Red Cross. He and a German-Jewish dentist were allowed in to see us; the former bringing messages and letters from the outside world, and the latter, keeping our teeth in some semblance of repair. The song, to the tune of "The British Grenadiers," went as follows:

> Once some talked of 'vacuation and some, I'm also told,
> Of hostile transportation to Peking's temples old,

But whatever information may reach the distant hill,
We're here in concentration, and bright and happy still.

Some talked of Nagaoka and some of Mr. Wang,
Of Chong Shan or Masaway, they gossiped loud and long;
But of all Chefoo's great heroes, there's no one to compare
With the valiant Mr. Egger, who brings us words of cheer.

Some talked of far Lourenco, and some of bare Cathay,
And some of Shanghai's compounds; so we didn't know what to say,
But of all the world's great places there's nowhere with such a thrill
As living in small places on Chefoo's Temple Hill.

The history of Temple Hill is perhaps best preserved in the poems and songs that the staff made up and which we all enjoyed and sang with gusto:

BUSINESS AS USUAL

You may reside at Nottingham,
Or even Timbuctoo,
At Singapore or Amsterdam
Or possibly Chefoo;
But one thing can't escape you—
It's come inside the door—
You know it and you feel it
That everywhere there's war.

Chorus:
So vitamin or vytamin
It does not matter which,
Take A to Z variety
And fill that empty niche.
We're rationing for victory
And victory's on the way.
It may be slow in coming
But it's certain as the day.

We may be short of butter,
But a substitute is found
In Vitamins—Peanuts

Minced, Mangled, Sliced or Ground.
The price of food is soaring,
But the Chinese chow is cheap;
Just try the native *tou-fu*—
Completely fit you'll keep.

The Staff are all in training
As table boys and cooks;
The men with brush and dust pans
The ladies cookery books.
The girls they lay the tables,
The boys they sweep the floor,
The prepites eat their rations
And never sigh for more.

The schools are running just the same;
The boys are running too,
And Desterhaft has won the mile,
The record broken through.
The goats reduced in number
Still yield their lactine juice
The hens on wartime rations
Still patronize Jean Bruce.
                    —Stanley Houghton

Four notable beards were prominent in Temple Hill. Two
came into camp with their owners: retired missionaries Mr.
Herbert Taylor, who lived in a third compound for retired missionaries and the foreign business community, and Mr.
Jennings, in his seventies. The other two beards were grown in
camp. One belonged to Goopy, who let his whiskers sprout, as
he was in charge of getting the stoves and hot water ready at an
early hour each morning. The fourth beard flourished from
necessity as Mr. Harris, who was in the same house as we
were, lay bedridden for many weeks following a fall from a
ladder. He was affectionately called "B," the result of oft-
repeated advice to his classes to "be" this and "be" that. These

beards were immortalized for us in the "Song of the Cactus," written and presented by Mr. Houghton and some of the senior boys with plenty of animation that had us in stitches:

SONG OF THE CACTUS

1. The San boasts many people
   But only one with beard;
   He potters round the boxes
   And many a plant has reared.
   The golf balls fall around him
   When he is out alone
   He hides behind his whiskers
   To avoid the danger zone.

Chorus:
   Oh they're always in the way,
   The goats eat them for hay,
   They have such spikes like cactus plants
   And lengthen every day.

2. Oh Miss Jennings, she was hungry,
   For she had nought to eat;
   She took her Papa's whiskers
   And called them shredded wheat.
   The B.S., they were jealous
   For they had none with beard;
   Bold Goopy copied cactus,
   And everybody cheered.

3. Bold Goopy he was stoking,
   And all the stoves he cleared;
   He stumbled o'er his whiskers
   And straightway singed his beard.
   The Prep School keep their champion
   In secret place you see,
   But when he shows his whiskers
   You'll know it's Mr. B!

4. So here's to cacti noble
   The trio with the beard;
   Who follow their example
   Will certainly be cheered.
          —Stanley Houghton and San Boys

Although letters were very infrequent, batches of mail did reach us and likewise got through to our parents in the remote regions of Free China. The chain of miracles that brought them was different every time. What a boost they gave to our spirits as they brought comfort and joy to us to know our parents were safe and well! But our letters to our parents meant even more because they knew we were in much greater danger. How encouraged one boy's parents were to receive this letter:

My Dear Mummy and Daddy,

I have just been sick a little but am well and happy now. Last Sunday we went to the diningroom and sang hymns, we had vilions (violins) and one boy came and blue on his trumpet. It was very nice. We are haveing sesame butter on are bread lots of times . . . . On Friday in the night it snowed very hard and in the morning it was very deep. We went out with are guloshers and coats and storm hats and overstockings, we had lovely fun . . . . Last week we had a con-set (concert), the boys sang about the kitchen and Mr. Buzer (Bazire) riecited (recited) the village Black Smith and Mrs. Buzer played the Moonlight Sonata it was realy two cats.

There is a stove where the Lower Ones have there class and the Transition and Upper One. Two Wendsdays A___ comes over from her compound and sees me and I go over from my compound to see her but I dont go two times.

With love from B___[2]

When any student or teacher was ill, it meant making special arrangements to try to give medical help as needed. One night Mr. Seaman was not well, and so Mr. Martin went to sleep in his room instead of Mrs. Seaman. In the middle of the night Goopy got up in the dark to get a drink. He could see the dim outline of a glass on the table and enjoyed what he found to be a very cold drink. There was even ice rattling on the bottom. In

[2]Sheila Miller, *Pigtails, Petticoats, and the Old School Tie* (Sevenoaks, Kent: OMF Books, 1981) pp. 142–143.

the morning he discovered it was the glass containing Mrs. Seaman's false teeth.

On the whole our time at Temple Hill was quite tolerable. While crowded conditions and lack of heating and sanitation were hardships, to be sure, the Japanese guards were not deliberately unkind.

Temple Hill was a far cry from the typical POW camp. In the first place, we were all civilians, and furthermore, many of us were children or teenagers. I don't think we ever lost the holiday-camp atmosphere of our experience, despite our many discomforts. What school child wouldn't jump at the chance of a Tom Sawyer-like existence where nothing was normal, particularly school work?

By summertime we really got in the swing of camp, as we got the chance to sleep outdoors—a relief from the overcrowding. Mattresses were lined up under the trees and mosquito nets were strung along above. As night fell, we looked up through the trees, awed at the clear panorama of stars overhead. The less poetically-minded stealthily played marbles and tipcat out of earshot of the teachers.

Part way through our ten months of internment at Temple Hill, Japanese Consular Police took over from the military authorities, and our situation improved a measure. The new commandant, Major Kosaka, allowed sand to be brought in for us to play in. He even let us have a supply of fireworks, so that we could have our own celebrations when festivities were going on around the temple with thousands gathering to worship the idols. The power of the big crackers really impressed us. Even a bucket thrown over one shot up as high as the top of the trees. I think I could still find the spot by the West wall where I buried one of my crackers, planning to retrieve it before I left the compound. Of course, when the day came, I forgot it in all the excitement.

With the coming of Major Kosaka as commandant, a little refinement seemed to come to our camp. We were now called a "Civilian Assembly Center."

Roll call, morning and evening, with all of us calling out our numbers in Japanese, became part of the daily routine. Mr. Martin wrote up the numbers in Roman letters for all of us to memorize. We were very quick learners, and those of us at the younger end of the school always ran out at the roll-call signal, to get to the front of the line. When the commandant in all his military braid and finery and with his attendant officers marched up, one of the soldiers with appropriate air-sucking preliminaries shouted out, "Bango," which meant "Number off!" Away we went, as fast as we could go: *"Ichi, nee, san, she, go, roku,* etc." The first four in the line-up could play a joke with the numbers. Instead of counting "Ichi, nee, san, she," we would sometimes say, "Itchy knee, scratch a flea." It gave us all a laugh, and since we said it so quickly, I don't think the Japanese knew what we were up to.

Sometimes after roll call, Major Kosaka would walk around among us. His quiet and dignified manner was a sharp contrast from the former military leader, who would flash a mouth of metal at us as he bellowed his orders. Major Kosaka had a kind face and talked to us in English, treating us with respect. "Here, let me hold it now," I shouted, as I took the commandant's long curved sword and swished it around in the air. He let the more daring among us also pull out his dagger with its ornately engraved handle and feel the sharpness of its point. "That's what they use to commit *hara-kiri* (ritual suicide) if they are captured, as it brings disgrace to the Emperor and shame on their nation to be taken prisoner alive," explained one of the more knowledgeable of our little group. He continued, "Their Shinto religion says the Emperor is God, and they are going to conquer the whole world."

Major Kosaka must have missed his own children at times like this, as the eager faces of ten-year-old boys looked up at him. And it must have touched him, seeing us all without our parents. He would smile at us, and there could have been tears in his eyes.

One time, with only a few of us round him and no soldiers in sight, he reached into the top pocket of his military uniform and brought out a little black-covered booklet. Eyes darting from left to right to make sure no one else was watching, he showed it to us—it was an English New Testament. We could see in his face he was one of us. We found out many years later that Dr. Hallam Howie of New Zealand, our school doctor, used to read the Bible to the major, and this was probably the copy of the New Testament given to him by Dr. Howie.

Though rumors of a move began to rumble around as the summer progressed, it was still a shock when it was actually announced that we were all to be transferred to a city about one hundred miles inland. The Japanese authorities had decided that all foreigners from Peking (Beijing), Tientsin (Tianjing), Tsingtao (Qingdao) and Chefoo would be interned in the one camp about two miles northeast of the old walled city of Weihsien. Since there was no railroad between Chefoo and Weihsien, it meant a journey by sea down the coast to Tsingtao first, and then a train trip.

Some of the Americans and Canadians were informed that an exchange with Japanese prisoners in North America was being worked out, and they would be repatriated soon after everyone was assembled at Weihsien. This party of Mission members and children left ahead of us to go to Weihsien. Their departure left 206 of us, of whom 140 were children, with no prospect of release in the foreseeable future.

Mr. Arendt, who still had his freedom, kindly notified our Mission leaders that we were being shipped to Weihsien. This was the German missionary who on a number of other occasions had risked his own safety during our ten months in Temple Hill by passing bags of rice and pieces of precious mail over the wall.

Major Kosaka went the second mile for us when he received the orders of our transfer. He himself took the two-day journey to the new camp to see what it was like. On his return he told us to take everything we could, as the conditions were much worse than at Temple Hill.

Once more our teachers and housekeeping staff faced the arduous duty of packing up. The commandant saw to it that all the cases, boxes, trunks and bedding bundles were loaded up in trucks and taken to the wharf, where all of it was stowed into the hold of the old cargo ship that was to take us. I was really excited about another move, and two days on a boat! What more could we have asked for except our freedom?

B ut when September 7, the day of our departure, came, I shared with all the others the fear of the unknown.

We had wakened early that morning and were huddled together in our upstairs room, all packed and clutching what we could carry with us. History was being repeated as we heard the shouts of the soldiers outside, and we knew we would shortly be herded out again and marched off. Miss Ailsa Carr, our Prep School Principal, then opened the Bible to Psalm 93 and read the first verse, "The Lord reigneth." Very quietly she described a picture of the King upon his throne. She told us, "We do not need to be afraid. God is our King, and He is in control." We were too young to understand it, but her life reflected Deuteronomy 33:12, "The beloved of the Lord shall dwell in safety by him, and the Lord shall cover him all the day long, and he shall dwell between his shoulders." After the teacher prayed, I looked up, and the fear of what might be ahead was gone. We marched out through the gate, met up with the Girls' School camp, and headed for the harbor, singing our chorus as before—"God is still on the throne."

On our departure one of the members of the school staff penned an acknowledgement to the Presbyterian Mission:

> We praise the American Board
> For the houses we've used, uninvited,
> Those houses so lofty and broad,
> On a hillside so sensibly sited.
> They have walls firm enough to withstand
> The gambols of youngsters rampagious,
> And gardens delightfully planned
> With poplars and fir trees umbragious.
> They have cellars too, spacious enough
> To receive all our luggage tremendous
> And the flour and the rest of the stuff
> Which our gracious custodians send us.
> So we thank the American Board
> With regrets for our lengthy invasion
> More eloquent thanks we'll afford
> On a later, more joyful occasion.

The boat in which we were to travel was a wreck. We were all stowed into the hold on top of our buried lunch and luggage. The authorities had allowed us to order bread, which was to be our mainstay on board. But the baker had let us down and as departure time approached, he still had not shown up. The ship would not wait. We sailed with no bread! Then, inexplicably, when we got out into the harbor we dropped anchor. Seeing this, our bread supplier, who had been standing helplessly on the dock, commandeered a small boat and drew up alongside. Quickly he handed us the bread. It was still warm. To those who carried the responsibility of feeding us, it was a special evidence of God's loving concern for us and another demonstration of the CIM mottos: "Ebenezer—Hitherto hath the Lord helped us" and "Jehovah Jireh—The Lord will provide." Evelyn Davey describes the trip from Chefoo to Tsingtao:

> The journey took two nights and two days. The boat was desperately overcrowded, and the 200 children and teachers were assigned to the hold. The hatches were battened down at night and no one was allowed on deck. Two long, wooden shelves ran the length of the hold, and the children lay top-and-tail like sardines. There were no toilet facilities! However, missionary foresight had anticipated this, and each of the younger children was provided, as a piece of essential equipment, with one small enamel potty. Many of the children were seasick, and the nights were very long.

It was the season of the annual breaking-up storm for which Chefoo is famous. Rounding the promontory to travel south to Tsingtao was always a hazardous venture, but God in his providence gave us two days of calm. After it got dark and we were well out at sea, a few of us disobeyed orders and clambered up on deck out of the stifling heat of the hold. In the coolness of the night air we enjoyed the moonlight dancing on the water, a sight that was to refresh our souls for what lay ahead.

On docking at Tsingtao at dawn on the second day, we were taken to the train station. Major Kosaka was standing on the platform. Mr. Houghton asked us all to face the commandant and stand at attention, and we were glad to show that last act of respect for him.

Seven hours later, thirsty from having nothing to drink and covered in dust, we reached Weihsien. A lot of our baggage was lost or broken into en route, but gathering together all we could, we jumped from the train. We were given only two minutes to get everything off. The men and older boys threw all they could out of the doors and through the windows before leaping off themselves as the train took off again.

As we dusted off ourselves and our belongings, half-dazed from the abrupt exodus, we heard shouts from hustling guards, telling us to climb into the waiting open trucks and a few ramshackle buses. And soon our convoy was winding through the narrow alleyways of Weihsien and out through the south gate of the walled city.

Turning east, we passed a few slum-like villages as we bounced along the rough dirt road. After a mile or two high walls and fortified towers came into view, and beyond these some large buildings set among trees. With a screech of brakes we came to a stop in a cloud of dust. Peering ahead as the dust settled, we saw Japanese sentries standing guard with fixed bayonets. Behind them were high gray walls and two big wooden gates with an inscription above in Chinese, "The Courtyard of the Happy Way." We had reached Weihsien Concentration Camp.

Chapter 6

WEIHSIEN
CONCENTRATION
CAMP

"Victory at all costs, victory in spite of all terror,
victory however long and hard the road may be;
for without victory there is no survival."

—Winston Churchill, Speech, House of Commons, May 13, 1940

One of the first arrivals had described Weihsien as follows: "Bare walls, bare floors, dim electric lights, no running water, primitive latrines, open cesspools, a crude bakery, two houses with showers, three huge public kitchens, a desecrated church and a dismantled hospital, a few sheds for shops, rows of cell-like rooms, and three high dormitories for persons who are single." It was to this scene of destruction and despair that we now came in September of 1943.

Weihsien had seen happier days. In the early years of the twentieth century the American Presbyterian Mission had established a school, seminary, and hospital there, with a number of large, American-style homes for missionary doctors and teachers. In fact, two Americans, later to become famous, were born in Weihsien—Pearl Buck, the popular writer, and Henry Luce, the co-founder of *TIME* magazine. When the "Courtyard of the Happy Way" was under the Presbyterians' control, it was a very pleasant and well-planned campus.

When we straggled into camp some thirty years later, however, the scene was quite different. The Japanese had taken over the foreign residences for their quarters. The rest of the compound suffered badly from looting and neglect. Running up from the high wooden gates at the entrance to the camp was a dusty black cinder road we called "Main Street." To the right and left, in an area measuring some 150 by 200 yards, were crowded over sixty assorted buildings. Besides an Edwardian-style church and classroom buildings were row upon row of long, low huts with small rooms measuring 9' x 12'—intended originally for students.

Into this motley collection of very run-down buildings about fifteen hundred of us were to be stuffed like sardines. We trudged in and up the sloping dirt road that was the main street of the camp. Internees came from all corners of the camp to "welcome" us. Near the head of our column, his white beard thrust forward as he leaned on his sturdy walking stick, was Herbert Taylor, already a pioneer of over sixty years in China. He was the eldest son of Hudson Taylor, the founder of the China Inland Mission, the parent mission of the Chefoo Schools.

We noticed in the camp quite a lot of children, who gave us smiles that seemed to say they understood what we were coming to. We later made good friends of many of them, most students from the Peking and Tientsin Grammar Schools, which carried on as did our own Chefoo School in camp.

That first day we were led to the open area to the west of the Mateer Memorial Church, which was beside the main street, not far from the main gate. After the guards checked to see that we were all present and correct, and after they read the camp rules and regulations to us, we were allotted rooms or dormitory numbers. Families of four were given one tiny room while those with six members usually managed two rooms. The rooms were practically bare, but after our baggage arrived a week later traces of personality began to appear. Many people's baggage was stolen en route or arrived badly damaged. Nevertheless, through the ingenious efforts of those with handyman skills, makeshift furnishings gave an amazingly homey appearance to our new quarters.

We younger children and our teachers were assigned to Block 24, one of the large buildings of classrooms. The only accommodation that could be spared for us was two rooms in the basement. We deposited what we were carrying, wondering how ever we would all be able to sleep in such a small space. There was no time to solve the problem as supper was ready at kitchen number one. The menu was onion soup, dried bread and pudding made with flour and water. As a special treat for new arrivals sugar was included. We were so hungry we thought it was a good meal.

Back at Block 24 we were asked if we wanted to have showers. This was a luxury we had never experienced before. While the experience of having showers in public, twelve at a time, was too big a shock for some of the staff and girls—at least for the first night—our gang of boys had a great time careering around the shower room as if we were on a skating rink.

Though the way back to Block 24 was fairly straightforward, the spirit of adventure was too much for me, and I decided to wander off alone to the other side of the camp to explore what

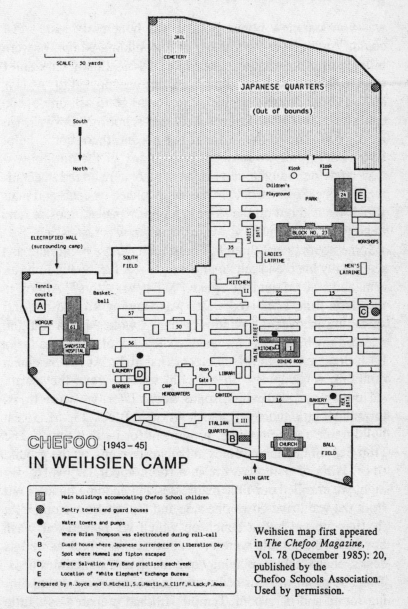

CHEFOO [1943–45]
IN WEIHSIEN CAMP

Main buildings accommodating Chefoo School children
Sentry towers and guard houses
Water towers and pumps
A Where Brian Thompson was electrocuted during roll-call
B Guard house where Japanese surrendered on Liberation Day
C Spot where Hummel and Tipton escaped
D Where Salvation Army Band practised each week
E Location of "White Elephant" Exchange Bureau

Prepared by R.Joyce and D.Michell, S.G.Martin, N.Cliff, H.Lack, P.Amos

Weihsien map first appeared in *The Chefoo Magazine*, Vol. 78 (December 1985): 20, published by the Chefoo Schools Association. Used by permission.

was now our new home. Soon I was hopelessly lost, and I couldn't remember the number of the building where we were billeted or even what it looked like. It was already dark and I tried to think which building my sister was posted to. At last, on the verge of tears, I plucked up courage to ask one of the camp residents if he knew where our school group was. He kindly took me to the hospital but no one there could help. Eventually, after we roamed round many of the buildings, I was safely delivered to the teachers, who were already becoming anxious. Some people in the camp loaned us coats and mats which we laid out on the floor in a tightly packed mosaic, and in no time a roomful of very tired children was fast asleep.

Some hours later I thought I must be having a nightmare as I put out my hand and felt an arm which was far too big to be an arm, and I called out half awake, "Whatever's this?" Almost at the same time I realized water was flowing around me and splashing in over the window ledge. I woke with a jolt and realized my hand was on someone's leg, not his arm, and that a flash flood had hit the camp on our first night. As our basement domicile was rapidly filling with water, I gave the alarm.

Things improved when, some weeks later, we were transferred to a little more spacious housing in Block 23, the largest building on the compound, prominent for its bell tower. The Prep School had three rooms at the western end on the ground floor. Nine of us boys were in a room about 12' by 16'. By night we unrolled our little mattresses and bedding bundles out from the wall, five down one side and four down the other. At the far end we had a bench on which we placed our wash bowls. In the middle were our cabin trunks, which served as desks, chairs, tables, playing equipment, and sometimes beds. This one room was our bedroom, classroom, living room, dining room, and playroom. Temple Hill had prepared us a little bit for lack of space but the conditions in Weihsien were much more cramped than Temple Hill had been.

At one end of our room, in due course, we had a little mud-brick stove built. The nuns had kindly given us a kerosene tin for an oven, making ours the most modern stove in the place! In this little stove we burned whatever twigs and wood we could gather and also our handmade coal-balls of coal dust and clay pressed together. Some of the more sophisticated in camp with entrepreneurial talent developed coal-ball making equipment out of an empty can with a stick attached to it. The deluxe model had two cans attached to the one stick. These little coal bricks could often be seen drying in the sun in the few square feet of private space people could call their own backyards. We heard a story of one family who "scrounged" bricks and a few other materials and achieved what every room aspired to—a little stove to keep out the winter cold. Evelyn Davey describes the following incident:

> One day the word got around that the guards were coming to look for stolen bricks and unofficial fires. One family hastily took down their stove-pipe, flung a blanket over the stove and sat on it. When the guard entered the room, smoke was billowing gently from under the blanket and it was getting HOT. The Japanese, either kind-hearted or blind, glanced around perfunctorily and passed on down the block.

Within a week of our arrival a number of Americans and Canadians left camp. They had been selected to be repatriated on the *Gripsholm* in exchange for Japanese prisoners. A number of these were from our Mission. Mrs. Hanna with Grant, Bruce, and Roxie were among the Canadians repatriated, along with Jack Bell. The other Bell children, however, had to stay behind in camp. The Waltons and Whipples were two of the American families I remember seeing leave. Perhaps it was because they were complete families that I felt my isolation more.

The day of departure for those being repatriated was one of mixed feelings for us all. For those going it was hard leaving behind old friends, who had been associates in missionary work or in business. For us in school it meant saying good-bye to a lot of our classmates. We were left with a very forlorn feeling as we waved good-bye to them from our perches overlooking the wall, wistfully watching the trucks move off. As our captivity extended from months to years, the sight of that exodus on September 14, 1943, lived on vividly in our memories.

At a later date the Japanese authorities, under pressure from the Red Cross, did arrange for children whose parents were interned in prison camps in Shanghai to be reunited with them in Pootung (Putong) and Lunghwa (Longhua) camps. In that transfer a number more Chefoo children left.

As people realized that internment could go on for a long time and that the quality of camp life depended on their own efforts, they got down to work. The Japanese limited their own involvement in the internal work of the camp, stating that their two responsibilities were to see that none escaped and to supply coal and wood for cooking and heating and "adequate" food. Adequate was an overstatement, as their basis for calculation was quantities for two meals a day.

Weihsien was really a world in microcosm with at least fifteen nationalities represented. The majority were families associated with foreign business enterprises, but the largest occupational group were missionaries, belonging to various Protestant mission boards or denominations. There were 400 Roman Catholic priests and nuns, although all but 30 of the priests were transferred to Peking not long after our arrival. Their going was a great loss to the camp work force as our school was a poor substitute in terms of manpower. Other people who carried the work load realized that with our coming, the ratio of children to the total camp population had risen to about one child to two adults, entailing heavier duties for older people. But since we were all civilians, we fared better than the military POWs. We were even given freedom to organize our own activities, being for all practical purposes a self-governing community, with committees elected by internees.

Camp was managed by nine committees: Supplies, Quarters, Employment, Engineering, Discipline, Medical, Education, General Affairs, and Finance. The senior ruling body in camp was called the Discipline Committee. The chairman was Ted McLaren of Butterfield and Swire, a British business concern with a long history in China. That committee was made up of a number of business people and missionaries, including some of our own staff. They were the group who spoke on behalf of the camp to the Japanese rulers and also were our mouthpiece to talk with Mr. Egger, the Swiss Consul, who was given permission on rare occasions to visit the camp.

Every able-bodied person was given regular work to do. In the kitchen most people worked a twelve-hour day shift and then had two days off. Many of the older boys took turns at pumping water up into the water tower for the camp supply. We younger children did things such as transporting water from one side of camp to the other and carrying the washing, which our teachers had tried to scrub clean, often without soap or brushes. We also sifted through the ash heaps to try and find pieces of coke or unburned coal, and gathered sticks and anything else that would burn, to try to keep warm through the winter. Undetected by the teachers or Japanese soldiers, we sometimes sneaked into the Japanese part of the compound and climbed the tall trees looking for dead twigs or branches.

We children learned to amuse ourselves with simple activities. Because one game we invented required buttons, it wasn't long before our clothes were pretty well all buttonless. Stringing the buttons on lengths of string, we spun them round, producing all sorts of variatons in their gyrations. One day a teacher picked up 26 buttons off the floor.

It was really amazing what value became attached to such simple possessions. I remember one Christmas receiving a grubby old cotton spool, and you would have thought I had been given a bicycle!

Walking became a favorite pastime. Some of us were able to boast of having walked a grand total of 63 miles. An elaborate wall chart recording our scores was our pride and joy.

We were grateful to the Roman Catholic sisters, who lived in another part of Block 23, for they kindly gave us wax to make our own candles. We treasured our homemade candles, made with one, two, three or even four wicks. We used them not only for telling stories by candlelight after the teachers were in bed, but for sizzling the ubiquitous bedbugs that crawled out of the walls and into our beds on the floor. Our four-wick candles were best for frying up old bread crusts "scrounged" from one of the kitchens. We also put them to work when we found mushrooms which made a rare delicacy fried in peanut oil. Our favorite trick was to take our candles with us to our hide-out at the bottom of the water tower near the hospital.

Our secret rendezvous spot was our delight until we were caught red-handed there with our candles one day by one of the teachers. Our punishment was "six of the best" on our behinds from Pa Bruce and a stern lecture from one of the businessmen who served as camp Fire Officer. We were terrified as he threatened that we might have to walk up and down in the camp with sandwich boards on our shoulders declaring that we were fire bugs and a menace to the community. Fortunately we were let off that punishment.

Sometimes we would climb out of our windows after the teachers in the next room were asleep and roam free at night. We had to watch carefully that we didn't disturb the guards or their watchdogs. We usually went out in gangs, as little boys like to do. I was the oldest among the nine of us boys who formed the youngest group of internees.

Boyhood rivalry was strong, and the leader of another Chefoo group, who was only three weeks younger than I, confronted me one time, saying, "I'm gonna be the boss of the whole gang." Some of my trusty henchmen buckled under and deserted me, but a small band remained loyal to me. I was to need the support of this little band a few days later when the worst of our frequent encounters took place. Just after roll call, the rival leader threw my ball away, very close to the Japanese soldiers' compound. "You go fetch it," I said, "or else . . ."

"Make me," came the reply.

"All right, I will." Soon we were tumbling on the ground, even rolling down a bank, taking turns to be in command of the struggle. After some minutes I got on top and rained down punches furiously, getting back almost as much as I was giving. Suddenly the shouts of defiance turned to screams and yells. I thought they were "put on" and so kept on hammering until I realized he wasn't kidding. I rose slowly to see the arm of my adversary dislocated at the elbow, with the bone sticking out at a gruesome angle. One of the doctors was able to slip the bone back into position and the arm recovered in due course. I got a hero's admiration from my gang, but lost my girlfriend and got the reputation from the girls of being a bully. Privately I think I felt quite justified. Even at the level of wartime existence, a boy's got to keep his self-respect!

The camp population included a variety of professional and vocational groups. We had a number of doctors, nurses and pharmacists who staffed the hospital, although equipment and medicines were at a premium. The educators among us established another smaller school, set up apart from the Chefoo, Peking, and Tientsin ones. Desperately short of paper, much of our school work was done in pencil and erased so that the paper could be used again. We used slates balanced on our knees for much of our school work. As the camp had some of the finest intellects in North China, we had adult education, special lectures, classes in several languages, art, history and other subjects.

Without music camp life would have been unbearable. A choir under Mrs. Bazire of the CIM gave concerts which included everything from Gilbert and Sullivan to Bach, with major performances being *The Messiah*, Stainer's *Crucifixion*, and *Olivet to Calvary*.

Also among the internees were some entertainment groups which were part of the Western community in the big cities in North China. A black jazz band added quite a bit of life to camp. In fact, for us younger children from Chefoo, who had known nothing but a very sheltered missionary environment, it was our first sight of a black person! And to come face-to-face with glamorous models wearing lipstick and high heels was mind-boggling!

Food and freedom were probably the major topics of conversation. The camp was organized into three kitchens, staffed by internees. Hands that were totally unaccustomed to the culinary arts were soon turning out fancy-named items which appeared on the daily menu board. These mysterious products completely belied their humble origin from turnips, eggplant and cabbage with occasional squid, fish or what could aptly be described as "no-name" meat. Actually, it had a name—it was either horse or mule. Morning, noon and night we lined up in long queues for our portion of food and then sat down at rough-hewn tables and benches. Servers had to try and be scrupulously fair, or there were complaints.

A typical camp menu would be: **Breakfast**—two slices of bread (often hard and flat if the yeast supply was low) and millet or sorghum porridge, with sugar on very rare occasions; **dinner or lunch**—hash or stew including mushy eggplant, popularly called "S.O.S." ("Same Old Stew"), and occasionally dessert; and **supper**—usually soup, which was often a watered-down version of S.O.S.

"As the diet was lacking in calcium (no milk, no cheese, no ice cream)," Evelyn Davey remembers, "we collected the shells from the black-market eggs, ground them into a powder and fed it to the children by the spoonful. We also gathered certain weeds around the compound and cooked them into a spinach-like vegetable to supplement the rations. Fruit, apart from a few apples, was almost unknown, and one little girl in school asked, 'What is a banana?'"

Second helpings of anything were very rare. When one five-year-old discovered that she was allowed a second drink of water at playtime, she shouted excitedly to the others, "Hey, everybody, seconds on water!"

However, there were times of feast as well as fast. Each Christmas special items that had come in through the Red Cross were saved up and used to provide something special. Mrs. Lack on our school staff, wanting to make the Chefoo Foundation Day occasion one to be remembered, pled the children's cause to the Japanese, and her pleading brought results, with the supply of extra flour. With a number of the other staff ladies helping, they mixed up Chinese dates, sugar, peanut oil and flour and managed to produce about 88 pounds of cake.

Encouraged with this success, the ladies attempted even wedding cakes! At least two of our staff got married in Weihsien Camp—Ruth Greening married Buddy Price; and Jeannie Hills married Joe Cotterrill. They had met each other for the first time in camp. This is how Mrs. Lack describes her cakemaking enterprise:

> We made up our minds that as the cake was about all we could give, we would give our best. One hundred and fifty guests were invited, including all children in the Senior School . . . Everyone made contributions. I also collected apricot stones from people who had been fortunate enough to get a few apricots, and these made lovely almonds. Also bits of orange and pumelo skin, some nearly two years old, were added. It grated up beautifully and gave the flavor which was all that mattered. We managed to collect two pounds of sugar altogether for this special cake, using a quarter of it for the cake and the rest for icing purposes. With a few real sultanas from our Red Cross parcels and a little dripping given me from one of the kitchens, plus oddments of spice and cinnamon, we set about this cake-making with a professional feeling. Lots of Chinese dates helped to make the mixture sweet. The tins were anything except cake tins, but we managed to get three sizes of right proportions, including a powdered milk tin for the top tier. The baking took five hours in a kerosene tin oven. The decorations were made from silver paper or tin foil. The pillars of wood were covered with tin and then polished. Someone lent a cake icing outfit and with some persistence we managed to make a boiled icing work for decorations. The ornament on the cake, a Gothic arch, I made from a strip of tin released on opening a tin of milk. This was covered with white tape and lily-of-the-valley, (a bunch of artificial flowers I had worn for five summers), with little bits of green here and there and with little bells hanging on the top gave it the finished look. The children loved pre-

paring for the wedding, and we all looked upon it as a jolly good excuse for a cake.

What a celebration it was too!

At one point during the war there must have been a real breakthrough in negotiations as arrangements were made through our home governments for "comfort money" to be made available. A sparsely garnished canteen enabled us to get eggs, peanuts, peanut oil and sometimes even apples and some other items, but prices were very high. Eric Liddell, patently a true Scot, was sitting in a chair outside the canteen on one of the rare times when apples arrived. He remarked, "Well even if we don't have the money to buy them, we can at least enjoy the smell." As the war progressed, commodities at the canteen and the food rations allowed in by the Japanese diminished drastically. Through the good offices of our indefatigable Mr. Egger of the Swiss Consulate, occasional parcels of food or medicines from friends in other parts of China were passed by the Japanese authorities and given to those to whom they had been addressed, to the envy of all.

In July 1944 a consignment of two hundred parcels from the American Red Cross were delivered for the two hundred Americans in the camp. We all crowded round with our mouths watering to see these privileged owners unpack undreamed-of delicacies in the form of tins of butter, powdered milk, coffee, salmon, Spam, and packages of raisins, cheese, chocolate and sugar. Out of their largesse we all benefitted by some tokens. That night in our room, our little gang of nine boys brought out the hoarded treasures and, by the light of the candles we had managed to keep secret, took a few leisurely savored nibbles before squirreling away the rest for the bleaker days we knew were coming.

About seven months later, long after the food from the parcels had disappeared and when winter was at its coldest and dreariest, a commotion erupted near the main gate. Fourteen donkeys were seen struggling to ascend the slope up the main road pulling their rickety carts, loaded high with food parcels. On each was clearly visible, "American Red Cross." The Americans were ecstatic while everyone else was glum and "choice" words about the Red Cross of every other country represented in camp were flying freely. When all the parcels had been unloaded and counted, there were found to be 1,550 —more than enough for every one of the 1,450 of us in camp. The commandant made a very fair decision, most people thought, by allocating one each to everyone and an extra half-parcel to the two hundred Americans.

The lineup for the parcels began bright and early the next morning, but young and old after long hours of waiting were greeted by the baleful news that there would be no distribution at all. Soon it was learned that seven of the Americans, very disturbed that American parcels would go to non-Americans, thus depriving them from getting seven and a half parcels each, had protested the commandant's directive.

Caught unprepared for a problem of this nature among the internees whose culture and customs had him baffled, the commandant, feeling obligated to present a minority's cause, relayed the facts of the problem to Tokyo for a judgment. The image of all the Americans was badly blemished as, predictably, tensions mounted daily in the camp.

After some days a pronouncement came from the Japanese authorities that there would be one parcel per person. The extra hundred parcels would be sent back for distribution to American prisoners in other camps.[1] It was the nearest we came to an

[1]Langdon Gilkey, *Shantung Compound* (New York: Harper & Row, 1966)). Chapter VI.

international crisis, but in due course feelings died down, and everyone was grateful for what had been received.

Our school was able to make very favorable exchanges of all the packets of cigarettes for nourishing food that kept us going through the winter. Not a mouthful of food was ever wasted. Without doubt the hardest weekly mouthful for me, until supplies ran out, was the spoonful of cod-liver oil that looked and smelled like slimy green marmalade.

Back in our room after our lessons one afternoon, John Birch climbed up onto David Allen's shoulders so that he could reach the top of the cupboard which stood behind the door. Birch, who slept on the floor in the opposite corner to me, was pressing a swallowtail butterfly under the heavy China bowl on the top shelf of our one and only cupboard. In the bowl was our whole Prep School allotment of highly treasured Chinese treacle, and below it, stacked on every shelf, were all the plates and dishes we possessed.

With a mighty heave, Allen, who was the strongest of us all as the teachers well knew, lifted Birch a whole foot higher. In that instant he lost his balance and grabbed for the side of the cupboard. Over it came, bringing the crockery down with a crash that was strangely muted by the treacle engulfing them and the broken china on the floor.

For a brief moment the sense of loss was overwhelming. But in no time we were roaring with laughter at the sight of two teetering toffee apples, covered from head to toe in the sticky mess. Not wanting to let even a sniff be wasted, we descended on them like bees in swarm, scraping up and licking off every last drop on them and on the floor.

I know for sure that that butterfly never got into the collection. From that point on I felt a bit more forlorn as I stood by the hour in the lineup, meal by meal, with only half a plate and a very chipped small enamel pie dish to complete my table setting. I guarded these battle-scarred dining companions till the day of our parting. The plate I left behind in camp, and the pie dish I took even on board ship as I headed for Australia after the war.

As more months passed by and it became all too obvious that our internment would be for a long time yet, the clothing situation became more desperate. We boys went barefoot and dressed only in shorts for the summer months to make clothes go further.

Our teachers must have felt for us as they saw us running around barefoot through many months of the year. Miss Davey, in fact, put her thoughts to rhyme, thinking of idyllic settings far removed from our grim situation:

BAREFOOT

If I were blind and could not see,
I think bare feet would speak to me.
They'd feel the heat of sun-baked earth
And tell me of the spring rain's dearth.
They'd rustle softly through the grass
And speak of green, where rabbits pass.
They'd tread where pine-strewn needles lay
And tell me of the wind at play.
They'd paddle in a shaded pool,
And I would know 'twas silver cool.
They'd walk upon the cobbled way;
I'd see where folk had passed all day.
They'd pick a way o'er stubbled field;
I'd glory in the harvest's yield.
They'd sink into the golden sand;
I'd see the waves: the breakers grand.
They'd stand upon the cold, damp ground;
I'd know the freshness all around.

> If I were blind and could not see,
> I think bare feet would speak to me.

Even though our shoes were saved for the winter, by the last year some had to get by with layered cloth top nailed onto wooden soles. Before long, shirts and pajamas were made from old curtains and mattress covers, and even blankets were cut up to make trousers. "Prickly seat" became more common than prickly heat. Since tablecloths were rather out of place in camp and were a dispensable luxury, they were cut up for underwear. In a day when there was no such thing as colored underpants, I was glad I wasn't the boy that had an embroidered wild rose right on the seat of his briefs.

Our teachers carried a heavy work load with the laundry since there was very little soap, and what there was was very inferior. The brushes soon lost their bristles, and many a knuckle was bruised on the ribs of the washboards. White shirts became but a memory as no clothes were spared from the graying common to Weihsien garments. "Give us the soap, and we will finish the job" was an often heard slogan around the laundry tubs in a part of the hospital basement.

The laundry was one of our chores. Three days a week a dawdling line of the younger children could be seen weaving its way back from the hospital to our rooms in Block 23, with basins of wet washing on our heads or in our arms. One time I tripped and had to detour by the pump to give everything another rinse and wring-out before delivering the goods to the teachers for hanging out on the line.

Some days when we had to wait for the washing, a few of us who were either braver or more morbidly inclined would let our curiosity get the better of us. The laundry was near the camp morgue. When we knew there was a body in the morgue awaiting burial, we would lean in the small window at the back, and using a long stick to lift a corner of the sheet, see who it was that had died. The room was fairly dark with only the one small window, and one time, just as the stick was making contact with the sheet, a man opened the door and the edge of the sheet fluttered upward. We didn't wait to see any more and took off without looking back.

The Japanese soldiers' leniency was evident by the way they didn't barricade an air-raid shelter tunnel that ran under the tennis court by the hospital. One of the corner searchlight towers was within 100 feet, but the guards knew that we liked to use the tunnel as a hiding place and didn't want to spoil our fun. A huge boulder in the middle almost blocked the path, and I remember times when some of us had a pow-wow around it, imagining what it would be like to start digging towards the wall. None of us, however, was quite enterprising enough to do much more than make a start.

Sanitation was appalling; all agreed that the camp's Health Committee had one of the hardest tasks. The sewage system consisted of open cesspools, one of which was only yards from the side windows of our room. Gangs of Chinese coolies, with buckets hanging on each end of a pole across their shoulders, came in each day to fill up and splish-splash their way up to the gate and out to their little fields, where they ran a thriving night-soil operation. The fetid stench floated in the kitchen-dining hall area where we were eating, or on hot summer nights it hung low over the camp in sultry, pungent clouds.

All water had to be pumped up into water towers and then relayed to kitchens and showers. Though the camp Health Committee decreed that all water for drinking must be boiled, disease was prevalent nonetheless: malaria, dysentery, hepatitis, and mental breakdowns all took their toll.

The medical accomplishments of camp personnel were remarkable and courageous, taking into account the lack of facilities, equipment, and medicines. Doctors performed many major operations and numerous minor ones. During our twenty-five months of imprisonment 32 children were born, and 28 people died. Had it not been for the trojan efforts of the Red Cross in getting altogether unprocurable medicines into camp to us by the most creative means, we would have fared much more gravely. It truly was the goodness and grace of God in His loving, providential care of us, and many a time and many a person testified publicly to this.

Living in the cramped conditions of camp required much patience and consideration. The rules of one of the women's dormitories in Block 23, which had eleven people in a space about 25' by 15', were as follows:

1. Poker must be laid at right hand of stove.
2. Wood must not be dried in front of fire.
3. The axe edge must be turned away from the room.
4. Children must not visit in rest hour.
5. No "foreign body" must be put in the highway.
6. You must be in bed before "lights out" (10 p.m.).
7. Mats must not be shaken on the balcony.

Following the ringing of the camp bell each morning was the daily roll call in six areas of the camp. It was always a tedious procedure, but thankfully did not always last five and a half hours as happened the first time. The older people were allowed stools or deck chairs, and we children were able to play marbles once we had been counted.

We learned how to play "luncre" from the Peking and Tientsin Grammar School children. To the teachers' dismay and our discomfort, we learned more than the game of marbles. The teachers were shocked to hear us describe with great animation our latest exploits with the best " 　　　 " marbles in Wei-hsien Camp. We had added to our vocabulary swear words that didn't exist in our world in Chefoo School, though some boys seemed to have quite a penchant for remembering Chinese swear-words. Unfortunately, most of us lost the Chinese language we should have remembered, having learned to speak it quite fluently from Chinese playmates before we left home. At school we were not permitted to use Chinese, as a number of our teachers did not understand it.

One morning when our little gang was sauntering back from our morning roll call on the small field in front of our building, one of my friends called out with great excitement, "Quick, come down to the main gate." As we ran after him, he shouted, "There's been fighting outside, and wounded soldiers are being brought in." We ran off as quickly as we could, hoping the teachers had not got wind of events in the direction we were heading. We thought it best to keep clear of the area of the gate as we could hear shooting in the distance. We didn't want to miss the action though, as we peered round the corner of the church building close to the front wall. We saw bandaged and bleeding Japanese soldiers limping in or being carried on stretchers. *We are really in the war now,* we felt. Typical of lively boys keen for adventure, we didn't have a thought for the teachers who on so many occasions did all the worrying for us. When the hubbub was all over and we got back, we were sternly rebuked for the danger we had put ourselves in and the concern we had given to others.

*O*ur teachers were wonderfully resourceful in the way they kept up our education right through camp. Three classes even took the Oxford Matriculation Exams. All sets of questions and papers were very carefully kept and after the war, back in England, were presented for assessment and were accepted.

We began Latin and French lessons while sitting on our cabin trunks. In later years I went on to teach Latin to the credit of my Latin teacher, Gordon Martin, and I can still say the Lord's Prayer in French—at least I believe that's what it is. I loved French, probably because it was my best subject. Unfortunately our French study was cut short abruptly when the teacher, Mrs. Lawless, died from typhoid contracted from the wellwater.

Some of our teachers helped to teach in the other schools organized for children in camp. Evelyn Davey taught at the kindergarten that was organized. She describes her pupils:

> The children were of many nationalities. Some of them were from missionary families; some from business families from Peking and Tientsin.
>
> Julienne was English. She was always the perfect lady. Her brown hair was swept smoothly back from her face, and her clothes were always neat. She never pushed. Her father was an executive of the Kaolan Mining Company.
>
> Jeannette was quick and volatile. She had a French father and an Italian mother. She spoke both languages, and also the Chinese dialect used by her *amah* [babysitter]. She learned English in six weeks.
>
> Margaret was a big five-year-old who liked to "mother" the others. She was Scotch and spoke with a soft brogue. Her father was a missionary of the British and Foreign Bible Society.
>
> Janet had the curliest hair, the brownest eyes, and the frilliest dresses in the class. Her daddy played in a dance band in Tientsin.
>
> Mickey Patternosta was Belgian. His favorite occupation was getting on top of a wall somewhere with some like-minded friends, and seeing who could spit most accurately.

I remember my teachers as missionaries in the finest sense of the word, sent in the place of my parents, who had work to do in a far-off part of China. I sometimes wondered how our parents would have coped with their children in the midst of fears and dangers of concentration camp life. As I think of the way that our teachers handled everything, I have great admiration for them and am grateful for the influence of their example in their self-control, serenity and courage. Three people who like me have such recollections of the teachers are the Taylors. They are great-grandchildren of our mission founder Hudson Taylor, and Dr. Jim Taylor is the present General Director of the Overseas Missionary Fellowship, which grew out of the China Inland Mission. Jim's younger sister, Mary Taylor Previte, writes as follows of her memories:

> The grown-ups in the camp knew enough to be afraid. I saw the war through the eyes of a child; an endless pajama party, an endless camp out. I entrusted my anxieties to my teachers in the belief that they would take care of us. Our teachers trusted God. . . . Our Chefoo teachers never watered down the standards for learning or decorum. There wasn't one set of standards for the outside world, they said, and another set for concentration camp. You could be eating the most awful glop out of a tin can or a soap dish, but you were to be as refined as the two princesses who lived in Buckingham Palace. The rules were clear: Sit up straight. Don't stuff food into your mouth. Don't talk with your mouth full. Don't drink when you have food in your mouth. Keep your voices down. Don't complain. After all, in Kitchen Number One, where we ate, Saint Paul and Emily Post ranked almost equal. We heard Saint Paul over and over again, "For I have learned in whatsoever state I am, therewith to be content." We were God's representatives in this concentration camp, our teachers said, and God was not represented well by rudeness. There was a gentleness about these steely teachers . . . .[2]

We did not have the option at Weihsien for pets, although in the heyday of the black market, the occasional live chicken with

[2]Mary Taylor Previte, "Legacy of Trust, *East Asia Millions* (Robesonia, Pa.: Overseas Missionary Fellowship, November/December 1985), pp. 102–104.

its feet bound came flying over the wall. However, of lesser breeds of living things there was a superabundance. These hordes were in the form of flies, rats and bedbugs. Only rarely did we encounter scorpions and their friendly touch!

However, the time I was stung by a scorpion was definetly a night to remember. To begin with, evening prayers had a special glow about it as Jennifer McLaren, the daughter of the Discipline Committee Chairman, had sat on a trunk between Philip Paulson and me. We were all of ten-and-a-half years old, and to have our shared girlfriend sitting between us was a rare treat. Later, with prayers over and visiting friends back with their families, we boys rolled out our bed rolls, and the lights were turned out. Outside all was quiet except for the guards marching past for the next change at the searchlight towers. Summer heat had brought the bedbugs up from the cracks in the floor, out of the mattresses, and in through places in the wall where chunks of plaster were missing. It was a particularly hungry night for the little critters, but we slowed them down considerably by pouring boiling water between the floor boards and into the holes in the walls. By our two- and four-wick candles we could see clusters of little black-red bodies scurrying across the sheets. The general consensus was that it was better not to see them; so we decided to retire, lying back somewhat nervously, as every little movement felt like it could be a bite in the making. One by one we nodded off to sleep. In the early hours of the morning I suddenly felt a stab like a needle going inches deep into my thigh. I leapt up in pain, and retreated limping to the safety of the trunks in the middle of the room. I had been stung by a scorpion. While some assured me that the scorpion was no more, I decided to spend the rest of the night lying on the hard trunks.

Another night of adventure in Weihsien that is very vivid to me was a cookout that the soldiers allowed us to have one night under the avenue of pine trees behind Block 24. Miss Davey, whom we called "Akela," arranged the outing for our little group of Cubs. Before we bedded down for the night under the stars, we got around in our Cub circle, and the Akela called out "DYB, DYB, DYB!" (Do Your Best) three times, and we responded, "We'll DOB, DOB, DOB!" (Do Our Best). We learned our Cub salute well. It was the salute using the index and second finger and in the form of a V.

That night provided one of the good memories of Weihsien for us. I can still feel the glow of being out under the pines and open sky and remember the oneness we felt as we sang together, before we nodded off, our Weihsien cub scout song to the tune of "'Till We Meet Again":

> By the blazing council firelight
> We have met in fellowship tonight;
> Round about the whispering trees
> Guard our Weihsien memories.
> And so before we close our eyes in sleep,
> We will pledge each other that we'll keep
> Scouting friendship true and deep,
> 'Till we meet again.

The next day during roll call, when the Japanese commandant was particularly belligerent and arrogant as he boomed out the orders, we furtively gave our Cub leader our "V-for-victory" salute and noticed that twinkle again in her dark eyes.

The noisiest nighttime entertainment by far came from the rats, of which there were a number of varieties. To try to cut down the menace of rats and flies, rat-catching and fly-catching competitions were organized. Some of the methods devised by the more innovative and competitive should have been patented. Norman Cliff and his cooperative of two other of the older Chefoo boys (Dick Vinden, who cut our hair, was one, I think) came in first, having caught and snuffed out 68 of the hungry beasts.

I cannot remember who was top fly-catcher, but some joked it could have been the boy of a Eurasian family in camp who had the misfortune to fall head-first into one of the cesspools. Happily his brother's frantic yells meant his sufferings were fairly short-lived. Help reached him after his fourth dunking, and to the great relief of all, "Cesspool Kelly," as he came to be called, was pulled out and revived. Fortunately he was the only cesspool casualty chronicled in Weihsien Camp's misadventures.

For a number of months, catching flies was the number one pastime in our spare minutes in lineups or when watching the ball games. My greatest feat was what I called my best Sunday catch—sixty-six during one Sunday school lesson! Although we younger children made quite a dent on the fly population, we didn't win the prize. We were outdone by the older boys whose methods of operation were on a larger scale.

The black market really was a lifeline to survival for many in camp. From the accounts that circulated in camp, the peak time of the clandestine purchasing of food and other necessities was in the first months of Weihsien Camp's history. The Roman Catholic fathers expanded their calling to include getting into the barter business. They acted as a conduit between people in the camp and collaborating Chinese outside, exchanging cash and valuables for eggs, bacon, fruit, jam and even chocolate. One method of collecting orders was for a Chinese, with his body blackened and greased, to shinny over the wall at night and pick up the "shopping list."

While doing this he would also arrange the time and method of delivery. Since the Japanese guards patrolled the walls constantly, the system called for great ingenuity.

Five of the fathers were Trappist monks. They had been forced to forego their vows of silence, having been put by the Japanese into one of the tiny rooms. Their joviality and good "works" became a byword in camp, and fortuitously their room was very close to the outside wall and made an excellent location for their food-smuggling enterprise.

One of these monks was Father Patrick Scanlan, an Australian of Irish ancestry. He became Chief Organizer of the underground food supply operation. He looked the perfect friar—in fact some called him Friar "Tucker" (Aussie slang for food). His long brown robes just seemed to match his red hair, rotund figure, and rosy complexion.

The chief egg supplier from the outside was a plucky little Chinese Christian lady called Mrs. Kang. At night, with the help of her little boys, she would funnel a steady flow of eggs into a drainage tunnel that came in underneath the wall near the priests' shack. If ever an egg business got cracking, this one did. Scanlan recorded all his dealings in what he called "The Book of Life." With his partners he carefully distributed the eggs and other food within the camp, making sure to escape detection by the guards.

Father Scanlan was very adroit in every aspect of the operation. One time when he was sitting on a stool by the wall, as was his daily custom, he had given the all-clear to those over the wall for the egg delivery to begin. Just then a guard approached. Quickly he had to stop putting the eggs into the bucket hidden under his robe and at the same time try to signal a halt to the flow coming under the wall. Unsuccessful in stopping the arrival of the eggs, he began to read his prayer book very loudly and then, in the form of a Latin chant, called his partners to come and help.

However, the guard was in an unusually talkative mood and decided to stop and engage him in conversation. In a few minutes the cracking of egg shells and the telltale mess of raw eggs streaming out from beneath his gown gave him away. With angry shouts of abuse, the sentry hauled him off to the guard house, where he was given a sentence of fifteen days in solitary confinement. When news of Father Scanlan's punishment got back to us, it was the joke of the camp. What was solitary confinement to one who had had twenty-five years of silence as a Trappist before internment?!

The priest was always one step ahead of the Japanese, and even in solitary, he put one over on them. After about a week, Scanlan was lonely for company. He decided to sing his prayers out loud in Latin, late at night. Since his cell was in one of the buildings housing the soldiers, his booming voice was keeping them from sleep. On hearing that these noisy activities were his obligatory religious exercises, they hesitated to interfere. They put up with the same routine one more night and then gladly sent him back to us. As Weihsien's egg hero was marched back into camp under guard, the Salvation Army band fell in behind them, playing a march and soon a long train of grateful mothers and children were part of the joyful procession. The Japanese appeared not to get the point as the camp feted its benefactor's return.

The black-market business was never quite as successful thereafter as the Japanese took much greater precautions. After a new commandant was appointed, it became even more difficult, and supplies were sorely missed. One Chinese was electrocuted while trying to smuggle in food; his body was left to hang on the wires as a gruesome warning to others.

Not long after, death touched us more personally. A young Greek with a powerful physique, admired by all of us boys as we watched him do his exercises, was caught stealing on one occasion and brought before the Discipline Committee. His punishment was to collect wood for the stoves for a week. One afternoon a small group of us were watching him at work on the upper branches of one of the tall trees, as suitable branches for burning had long since gone from the lower levels. He was swinging from a strong-looking bough as he jumped up and down on a dead-looking one below him, trying to break it off. All of a sudden, the top branch snapped instead, and he fell to the ground not far from us. People ran to help him straightaway, but the fall had injured him critically despite his great strength. He died the next day.

The boy's family was very bitter, cursing God in their tragic loss. It was so sad to us that they didn't share the hope that their son had found. Dr. Howie, our School Doctor, had led this young man to faith in Christ just a few days before he died.

A year before the war ended the reality of death came even closer to us. Brian Thompson was 16, the eldest son of one of our Mission directors. His mother and the rest of the family were all in camp together, but his father was at the Wartime Emergency Headquarters of the CIM in Chungking and was thus separated from them since the time of Pearl Harbor.

Brian was tall for his age and always full of energy. The start of the evening roll call was long overdue for the group that met on the old basketball court between the hospital and the corner searchlight tower. A bare wire that ran to the tower had sagged quite low, and some of the older boys started jumping up and just tipping it with the end of their fingers. "Whew, I got a shock off that," said one as his feet touched down again on the ground. Brian decided that he would try, but being taller his hand hit the wire and was pulled onto it by the current. It was summertime; he had no shoes on; the ground was damp. He fell, bringing the wire down with him, narrowly missing others as they stood in their rows. Quick-thinking companions held Brian's mother back from reaching him or the wire, or she too would have been killed. After a little while, others nearby hit at the wire with a wooden stool and freed him. The doctors, of which the camp had a number, ran over and applied artificial respiration until late into the night, but Brian did not recover consciousness.[3]

Our principal and Mr. Houghton led a very solemn yet triumphant funeral service the next day. The shortness of life and the reality of eternity were brought home to us with force as Pa Bruce related that Brian had missed the roll call in camp but had answered the one in Heaven. How important it was for us to sing and know "When the roll is called up yonder, I'll be there." That night we went to bed with sorrowful spirits. The black walls around us seemed somehow darker and higher. Yet, above us the camp had no roof to keep our spirits in. Above and beyond our fears and sadness our eyes looked upward to Heaven, which became more real to us than ever.[4]

[3]Norman Cliff, *Courtyard of the Happy Way* (Evesham, Worcs: Arthur James Ltd., 1977), pp. 92–93.

[4]Charles and Claire Mellis, *Missionary Discipleship: The Story of R. E. and Ella Thompson* (Farmington, Michigan: Missionary Internship, 1982), chapter 4.

Chapter 7

OVER THE WALL

"Stone walls do not a prison make
Nor iron bars a cage."
——Richard Lovelace, *To Althea, from Prison*

"Something there is that doesn't love a wall."
——Robert Frost, *North of Boston, Mending Wall*

rian's death had temporarily taken our gaze above the confining walls of our compound. Nevertheless, walls remained a fact of life for us at Weihsien. Our knowledge of conditions and events outside was severely restricted, and getting reliable news and information was a constant challenge.

We did know that the situation in 1944 was very complicated, with the area immediately surrounding Weihsien Camp under the control of Chinese puppet troops. The main Japanese garrison over these soldiers was at a city called Fangtze (Fangzi), on the railway about five miles southeast of our camp. Beyond this fifteen-mile radius of Japanese-controlled territory were Communist and Nationalist soldiers and isolated guerrilla units.

For a period of time the Japanese published a daily newspaper in English, edited by Germans in Peking, which came to us once a week. As paper became more scarce, however, issues decreased, and the size shrank to half a page. It was, moreover, nothing but a propaganda piece, designed to discourage us regarding the allies' war effort and give the impression that Japan was winning. But, from the names and places mentioned, those who were knowledgeable were able to deduce that the scene of the fighting was growing ever nearer to Japan, indicating that Japan was losing.

Obviously our half-page of weekly "news" was not to be trusted. We would have to find another source.

Among the large business community in camp were many who were experienced and successful in their own lines of business and well-acquainted with the general political situation in China. Courageously they put their abilities to good use in the camp. One of these men was Laurance Tipton,[1] an Englishman with a British-American tobacco company in China. Another was Father Raymond de Jaegher,[2] one of the Jesuit Fathers who, unlike the other priests, had not been moved back to Peking.

Father de Jaegher was Belgian and had worked more than ten years in China. Both fluent in Chinese, Tipton and de Jaegher became good friends in camp. One thing that drew them together was their common desire to hear news of the war's progress. To get such news into camp, they looked for ways of making contact with cooperative Chinese. What Father Scanlan had been able to achieve in the food-smuggling line, de Jaegher accomplished in the process of incoming and outgoing mail.

Unwittingly, the Japanese proved to be very helpful in this process. The earliest method that de Jaegher employed for

[1]Laurance Tipton, *Chinese Escapade* (London: McMillan and Co Ltd., 1949).

[2]R. J. de Jaegher, *The Enemy Within* (Bandra, Bombay: Society of St. Paul, 1952).

sending letters was to use Chinese-style envelopes addressed in Chinese characters. But a return address was needed, and this is where the Japanese proved an unknowing help to us. When they commandeered the compound they had not destroyed the hospital files. De Jaegher chose at random the Chinese names and addresses of former hospital patients, whose record cards had been overlooked by the Japanese. These now provided authentic Chinese return addresses.

The next step was equally critical. The letters had to be sent to friends of the internees who were either Chinese, German or Italian. Most were businessmen or missionaries living in Tientsin or other places in the northeast. Because Germany and Italy were allied with Japan, their citizens were allowed to send and receive mail unrestricted. Mail sent via them had much less chance of censorship than if sent directly to the CIM office in Chungking or to other "enemy" nationals in the country. Each envelope contained many enclosures for mailing on to others. Thus with Chinese envelopes, from Chinese addresses, written in Chinese script to allied nationals, the mail was better able to escape detection and was ready to be sent on its way.

Here, however, was another dilemma. There was, of course, no such thing as a corner mailbox, and making use of the Japanese-controlled local post office, where censorship was rife, was out of the question. While international accords demanded that the Red Cross be allowed to deliver mail to and from internees, letters had to be of standard length and were open for inspection by the Japanese. If our contraband mail could be passed on by hand, it would be much safer.

De Jaegher always had a way. At first he dispatched the mail by tying a packet of letters with an appropriate amount of money to a half-brick and then hurling the bundle over the wall to Chinese colleagues. As surveillance was tightened and more

61A

To The COMITÉ INTERNATIONAL DE LA CROIX-ROUGE,

GENÈVE (Suisse)

Please transmit the following message:

DEMANDEUR—ANFRAGESTELLER—ENQUIRER

PLEASE WRITE IN BLOCK LETTERS.

Nom-Name __MICHELL__ Nationality __BRITISH__
Prénom-Christian Name-Vorname __Dr WALTER JAMES__
Rue-Street-Strasse __CHINA INLAND MISSION__
Localité-Locality-Ortschaft __KUN MING__
Province-County-Provinz __YUNNAN__
Pays-Country-Land __CHINA__

Message à transmettre—Mitteilung—Message
(25 mots au maximum, nouvelles de caratère strictement personnel et
familial)—(nicht ueber 25 Wrote, nur persoenliche Familiennachrichten)—(not
over 25 words, family news of strictly personal character).

DEAREST	DAVID	HOPE	SEE	YOU
JOYCE	SOON.	WE	GO	FURLOUGH
RECEIVED	YOURS	AUGUST	HOPE	YOU
WELL	HAPPY	WE	WELL	LOVE
PRAYER	DADDY x	MUMMY x	JOAN X	BRIAN. X

Date-Datum __DECEMBER 1st 1944__

DESTINATAIRE—EMPFAENGER—ADDRESSEE

PLEASE WRITE IN BLOCK LETTERS.

Nom-Name __MICHELL__ Nationality __BRITISH__
Prénom-Christian Name-Vorname __DAVID__
Rue-Street-Strasse __CIVIL ASSEMBLY CENTRE__
Localité-Locality-Ortschaft __WEI HSEIN__
Province-County-Provinz __SHANTUNG__
Pays-Country-Land __NORTH CHINA__

ANTWORT UMSEITIG.   REPONSE AU VERSO
Bitte sehr deutlich schreiben. Prière d'écrire très lisiblement.   REPLY OVERLEAF.
Please write clearly
All messages to be written in English or if in any other language
an English translation must be attached.
PLEASE WRITE IN BLOCK LETTERS.

Sample of
one of the
Red Cross
letters that
David
received
from his
parents
while at
Weihsien.

E

electrified barbed wire entanglements were put in place, more sophisticated methods had to be devised.

Though the Japanese gradually whittled down the number of Chinese workmen they let into camp, the one group they were not in a hurry to replace with their own labor was the "cesspool coolie crew." De Jaegher, ever alert to possibilities for more fruitful contact with the outside world, volunteered to oversee this somewhat less-than-salubrious operation. He had the dignified title of "Sanitary Patrol Captain" and all that went with it in terms of olfactory side-effects. For quite a while some of these coolies acted as couriers and carried out packages of letters in their ragged cotton trousers. The guards at the gate kept well clear of them for obvious reasons.

However, when de Jaegher noticed one day that the soldiers at the gate had begun searching the coolies, he had to put his ingenuity to work once more. This time his solution was to have a craftsman in camp fashion a metal box with a watertight sliding lid. He would pack the letters carefully inside this tin and discreetly plop it into one of the full cesspool buckets, the tin to be retrieved outside. Later on even this method became too risky, and de Jaegher was left again to ponder how else to outwit the guards.

In the end de Jaegher hit on a very simple scheme: Official mail deliveries were made to the camp each Saturday. While the propaganda newspapers formed the bulk of this, some of the International Red Cross letters of the prescribed twenty-five-word length also arrived this way in little dribbles. By closely watching the mailman's movements, de Jaegher observed that the last thing he did after the final search by the guard was to put the empty mailbag into a small canvas bag fixed to the center frame of his bicycle. De Jaegher experimented by slipping a small bundle of letters with a dollar bill on top into this bag. As he had hoped, the man saw it and quickly looked around. De Jaegher, out of sight of the guards, beamed vigorously at the mailman, bowing and cupping his hands in the Chinese fashion to express thanks, and the mailman left the camp. Once outside the gate, our inconspicuous-looking letters were passed on to faithful Chinese Christians or other trusted contacts who would get our messages to the world outside. The system never faltered from that day on till the war was over, though it did have to be supplemented with other means as the mailman's visits got less frequent.

*T*he most outlandish correspondence to reach the camp during the war arrived in early May 1944. The Camp Administrative Committee kept the contents dead secret, as they knew chaos would otherwise have resulted. The letter in question was one written by the commander of Chinese Nationalist forces based in a northern part of Shantung province. He had a plan to fly in a fleet of planes and attack the Japanese. He would save all 1,500 of us, spiriting us away to freedom in Chungking in the far west, the seat of the Free China Government and the allied support forces.

The whole plan appeared to be the wild vision of an erratic leader who saw in this bold stroke his hopes for greater recognition. The impracticality, considering the many dangers and the condition of the sick and elderly, not to mention the high percentage of women and children, was evident to the committee. They responded cautiously, not wanting to lose the link with a potentially valuable ally, but at the same time not wanting to give the green light to a far-fetched scheme which they might be powerless to stop once it was launched.

The camp committee took Tipton and de Jaegher into their confidence to get their advice. The outcome of these discussions was that the two of them should try to escape from the camp so that they could meet the leader of this unit, who purportedly had an army of 60,000 soldiers.

De Jaegher worked through his cesspool coolie cohorts to acquire a good knowledge of the location and size of the military groupings in Shantung Province, and he and Tipton mapped out a course of action. To ensure the success of their escape, a number of things had to all work together. The guards, the moon, the place and time for rendezvous all had to be carefully considered, and there was no time to lose. June 9th or 10th, just ten days away, was chosen as the target date, as that night would give them an hour of darkness to make good their escape from the camp area before the moon's ascent.

It was necessary, too, to make the escape attempt during the duty period of the team of guards that were the most lax. This squad was on the 9:00 p.m. watch, and their routine began with an inspection up and down their beat by the wall and in their tower, followed by a ten-minute break for *ocha* (Japanese tea) and a smoke. In that short span of time, de Jaegher and Tipton concluded, they would have to make their escape.

Only three members of the camp committee knew the date the escape would be attempted, and all were sworn to secrecy. They agreed that de Jaegher should be allowed to tell his Superior, Father Rutherford, now that plans were definite and their escape kits were being prepared. Little knapsacks were packed with a few personal effects, plus a typewriter, a watch and fountain pen requested by the Nationalist soldiers.

Right at the last, Rutherford persuaded de Jaegher to back out of the venture because he feared there could be cruel reprisals on the rest of the camp, and he didn't want one of his priests being responsible for it. With great reluctance de Jaegher agreed. The organizing group of Tipton, de Jaegher, Roy

Tchou, and Tommy Wade asked Arthur Hummel, Jr., an American who had been a teacher in a school in Peking, to take his place. Hummel accepted without hesitation, and final preparations were given fine-tuning.

News had come through the "water-closet wireless" that a small band of Chinese soldiers disguised as peasants would be at the meeting place, two miles north of the camp, at the pre-arranged time. Every care was taken not to arouse any suspicion within the camp and, apart from accelerating their sun-tanning program, Hummel and Tipton carried on as normally as they could. The suspense for those in the know for the last few days was intense.

The watchtower chosen for the escape bid was the shortest one of the six around the walls. It was located in the middle of the west side, where a bend in the wall to the north obscured it from the searchlight tower beams. On June the 8th, Hummel and Tipton and the other three, including de Jaegher, did a dry run during the daytime. They got a good look at how to avoid touching the electrified wire while scaling the wall at the tower.

The next evening, while everyone else in camp was going about their humdrum routine in what, for many, had become an almost zombie-like existence, the scent of freedom was already in Hummel's and Tipton's nostrils, and their hearts were beginning to beat faster. As casually as they could, they let some-one in their respective rooms into the secret, asking them to do their best to cover for them, at least until the evening roll call, by which time they would hope to be safely at the Nationalist soldiers' headquarters.

By 8:00 p.m., as Hummel and Tipton slipped into their close-fitting black Chinese clothes that had been specially made and smuggled in to them, the others were closely monitoring the movements of the guards. At 9:00 p.m., the easygoing watch came on duty as expected. To Hummel's and Tipton's consternation, however, the tower guard didn't walk his beat straightaway as he usually did. The two would-be escapees waited breathlessly in the shadows for ten more minutes and then breathed a sigh of relief as the guard moved away from the tower. In a flash, de Jaegher, Roy Tchou, and Tommy Wade ran into the tower and helped Tipton and then Hummel up the wall and over the live and barbed wire fences.

Once on the other side, the duo retrieved the knapsacks that had been thrown over after them and ran to the overgrown Chinese graveyard some 100 feet away, throwing themselves down behind the first grave mound they came to. As they waited a few moments to catch their breath and get their bearings, they realized with much thankfulness that no alarm had been raised. They got up noiselessly and, after stumbling through the fields of millet, cautiously waded through the river that ran north of the camp. With the moon now shining, they headed off quickly for the rendezvous a mile and a half away.

Great was their relief on reaching the cemetery to find a mounted detachment in hiding, waiting with ponies to take them to their headquarters' hideout. Striking up friendly conversation with the soldiers, they traveled with them through the night, eventually reaching the unit base the following afternoon.

Meanwhile, back at the camp, de Jaegher and the others climbed down out of the tower undetected and then endeavored to retire casually for the night. De Jaegher's first concern on reaching his room was to pray for his compatriots' safety. At the next morning's roll call, Hummel and Tipton were not missed, but knowing their absence couldn't be concealed for very long, Ted McLaren, the chief of the Camp Committee, reported to the Japanese that they were missing. The commandant raged and fumed. Roll call was doubled to morning and evening, and food supplies took a further cut back—no meat, not even horsemeat for a while. But all of us were thankful that the Japanese response took the form of voluble haranguing rather than any physical punishment.

Eventually, however, the furor over the escape of the two men, who had achieved hero status in camp, died down completely. Nothing new seemed to happen to relieve the daily tedium. When some months passed with no news of Hummel and Tipton's whereabouts or of the war's progress, de Jaegher and his colleagues began to wonder if a worse fate had met their friends. One day, however, as de Jaegher mumbled the agreed-on password *wushi-liu* (56) while shuffling among the Chinese coolie work party, he got a nod of acknowledgment.

"Come to my 'office' (a modified latrine cubicle) so we can discuss the next job," de Jaegher called out with annoyance as he looked at this man. With the guard's suspicions satisfactorily allayed, the priest escorted the coolie into the cubicle. Once inside, the workman pulled out a tightly compressed note from the lining of his baggy trousers and, faintly smiling, handed it over to de Jaegher.

That night, when de Jaegher had decoded the message, he was hardly able to contain his excitement. At long last, proof had come that Hummel and Tipton had made it safely to freedom and that two-way communication was about to start. He let McLaren and Hubbard of the Camp Committee into the secret. A brief coded response was sent out in the same manner as it had come.

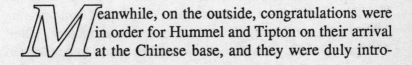eanwhile, on the outside, congratulations were in order for Hummel and Tipton on their arrival at the Chinese base, and they were duly intro-

duced to Commander Wang. They set to and prepared a report which was to be taken as soon as possible to the British and American embassies in Chungking. Typing it up was quite a delicate process. The typing was done on a thin white silk handkerchief stuck onto paper by flour paste. The report gave news of the camp, particularly stressing the urgent need for medical supplies and comfort money as well as a plea to quash any requests connected with the Chinese rescue proposal. They also stressed very strongly their concern for the safety of all in camp, should the Japanese in defeat order a transfer of all prisoners to Japan as hostages or even attempt a wholesale massacre.

Sewn into the soles of a pair of Chinese cloth shoes, the message, after many weeks and miles of hazardous travel westward, reached its destination in Chungking, still legible though very damp.

Through the yeoman help of Billy Christian, a former Weihsien prisoner, the greatly needed medical and other supplies were assembled. They were then flown by a B-24 and dropped by parachute in a location about fifty miles from Weihsien camp, where Hummel and Tipton were in hiding with the Nationalist soldiers.

As parts of a radio transmitter and receiver were damaged beyond repair in the drop, Hummel and Tipton had to wait several more months before replacement parts could be obtained from Chungking. At last the units were put into working order and the two escapees could begin in earnest to send back news to the camp, as had been their intention all along.

But if the radio suffered for its journey, the four boxes of medicines sent by the American Air Force from Chungking arrived intact. But getting them into the camp was another matter. Hummel and Tipton arranged for the four crates to be taken to our old friend Mr. Egger at the Swiss Consulate in Tsingtao, in the hope that he could get them into the camp.[3]

Though Mr. Egger was due to visit the camp to take in comfort funds that had reached him recently and also a small quantity of medicines that he was able to buy locally, he was absolutely nonplussed as he examined the four big boxes that were delivered to him. The shipment included the new sulfa drugs, the like of which were unknown in North China at that time. He identified medicine after medicine as ones that the Japanese authorities would never let through. He himself could never have got hold of them, and the Japanese certainly couldn't have obtained them from anywhere either.

Suddenly he had a brain wave. Calling his secretary, he had her type up on four pages of the Embassy letterhead the typical medical items that he could buy in Tsingtao—things like aspirin, antiseptic, etc. He instructed her then to leave a four-line space after each item. When this was complete, he signed the list and took it to the Japanese Consular Police for clearance.

At the police office there was momentary puzzlement at the unusual layout and waste of paper, but no real objection was raised, and the necessary seals for approval were stamped on each page. This hurdle past, Mr. Egger knew that the major one of getting the boxes by the camp guards still lay ahead of him.

Back at his office, Mr. Egger had his secretary use the same typewriter and, with a gleeful grin all the while, watched as she inserted the names of all the new medicines on the lines in between.

When he reached Weihsien camp the next day with his four big boxes and lists and presented them to the guards, they were completely bewildered. Everything looked in good order with

[3]Gilkey, *Shantung Compound*, Chapter IV.

the right seals stamped in the right places, but they were mysti-fied how approval could possibly have been given for such medicines for the camp. Egger was chuckling quietly inside as he saw them in such a quandary, feeling certain they would not refuse him with his papers so perfectly executed. They were baffled, but not wanting to lose face, they let him in and he handed over the life-giving supplies to the grateful doctors and nurses at the hospital. And so our tenuous over-the-wall lifeline survived one more strain.

As surveillance by the Japanese guards intensified, our faith-ful mailman could not come regularly enough to be reliable. More ingenious methods of sending messages had to be developed.

"*Pu-shing-te* (No good)!" the guard shouted one day in Chinese to the string of coolies as they paused to rest a moment and switch the poles car-rying their cesspool buckets to the other shoulder. "No daw-dling or talking to anyone," the guard growled as de Jaegher, keeping just out of sight of the guard in charge of the work crew, kept watching his messenger coolie closely. He watched the squad move off again with their half-jogging gait and sway-ing motion as they approached the corner of one of the build-ings. With the guard now round the corner, the coolie turned and, looking in de Jaegher's direction, spat into the dust.

As spitting was a way of life with coolies, the action passed unnoticed by anyone else, but de Jaegher's eyes were scanning the ground closely. Moments later, with the workmen and guard around the corner, de Jaegher, the picture of nonchal-ance, picked up the little pellet he could see lying in the dirt. With his heart pounding he went back to his tiny room, his hand gripped tightly around the coolie cargo. He unwound a piece of tightly folded rubber film to find a small sheet of silk with a typed message on it. How good it was to hear a little about Hummel and Tipton's experience, but most gratifying of all was to get for the first time news that was not just a package of rumors!

Over the next few days the news was very quietly circulated in camp. Those who wanted to have more detail were directed to one of the more private latrines, which doubled as reading room with the bulletin pasted on the inside wall.

Some of the cesspool coolies who helped us in our communications effort took very great risks which would have cost them their lives had they been caught. There were many close calls, such as the time a guard, during the routine search at the gate, forced the new coolie at bayonet point to open his mouth. With a gentle gulp he swallowed the pellet, and with it our latest news bulletin!

De Jaegher and Tchou realized they had to work fast when they saw what happened. One of them dashed to the hospital saying there was an emergency that he could not explain but that co-operation was imperative. He was given a little supply of castor oil with no further questions asked. After some conniving to evade the guards, they administered the medicine and up came the news right on time for the evening report.

Whether the news pellet was in the coolie's mouth or up one nostril (and blown out in the old Chinese nose-blowing style), our news dispatches got through. Through this circuitous route we heard reports from the war zones including the news of Germany's surrender.

For everyone it was hard not to let on to the Japanese that we knew that the war in Europe had ended. But for two young men in camp the news was too good to keep. On the night of May 7th, 1945, disobeying curfew, they climbed into the bell tower of our building, Block 23, and right on the stroke of midnight rang the camp bell.

Panic broke out. The Japanese sounded the alarm immediately, and within minutes angry guards were running by our window with their swords clanging as they headed for the main gate. Simultaneously a siren pierced the night air, signaling an escape attempt to the Japanese garrison a few miles away. Some among the internees, thinking the camp had been attacked, became hysterical.

The commandant thought he had a revolt on his hands. But when the swarms of garrison troops arrived and there was still no sign of resistance, he flew into a seething rage and gave orders for a complete roll call. So at 1:00 a.m. every one of us, from the youngest babies to octogenarians, turned out to be accounted for.

The sound of the bell was so loud in our building that I was sure it would have made some people fall out of bed. In our room we had nothing to worry about as we already slept on the floor. We were still trying to come to our senses when the guards burst into the building shouting, "Out! Out!"

Outside, while the earlier snow had all melted, frost confirmed that it was as cold as it seemed. We stood motionless in our rows with blankets draped round us while menacing guards stomped up and down the lines, glowering fiercely. Up on the low stage at the front, flanked by heavily braided reinforcements from the garrison, the commandant, whose nickname was "King Kong," for obvious reasons, bellowed and hollered in Japanese, oblivious of the camp interpreter's efforts to try to get in a word of explanation.

This went on it seemed for hours until some of the men in the back rows started to sing, "For he's a jolly good fellow." The situation could easily have turned very nasty. But, after a few more threats that serious reprisals would follow if the perpetrators did not own up, the commandant dismissed the parade.

Most people were very glad to get out of the night air and stumbled back to bed. Our Prep School group of fifteen eleven-year-olds, however, made the most of our midnight escapade. We leapt from the railing of the summer house in front of our building, holding our blankets up behind us as if we were coming down by parachute. We had our own version of Superman and Batman, long before we had ever heard of them. We thought the night adventure was terrific. Eventually, though, the teachers sent us back indoors to bed.

Next morning we felt the chance for sleeping in was worth more than the usual two slices of dry bread that was at the end of the breakfast lineup at kitchen number one.

As a school we put on our own celebration of VE Day by a display of "agility exercises" under Mr. Martin. A few weeks later the two responsible for ringing the bell came out into the open, and the Japanese accepted the explanation that they did it for a "dare." It would never have done if the connection of the incident with VE Day had come to light, as the Japanese would then have known for sure that we were getting news about the war.

The steady stream of two-way traffic in the news never ceased in spite of such setbacks. Reports left the camp the same way as they came: the message was typed in code on fine silk (made from cast-off underwear) and then encapsulated in rubber film. Everyone's spirits were lifted from knowing that somehow a lifeline with the allies had been successfully established. The "bamboo wireless" gave us contact with the world outside and kept up morale. The wall had been conquered.

Only in retrospect can we appreciate the ingenuity and sacri-

fice that went into that communications effort. Many cooperat-
ed, putting themselves in jeopardy to reach over the wall in order to bring us news and supplies. While practically none of us
knew at the time how all the miraculous events were coming
about, everyone was certainly grateful for them. The hearts and
voices of many were lifted up again and again in the hymn of
praise so well loved by the China Inland Mission:

> How good is the God we adore,
> Our faithful, unchangeable Friend!
> His love is as great as His power,
> And knows neither measure nor end!
>
> 'Tis Jesus the First and the Last,
> Whose Spirit shall guide us safe Home;
> We'll praise Him for all that is past,
> And trust Him for all that's to come.
>
> **—Joseph Hart**

Chapter 8

OF ALL THE WORLD'S BRAVE HEROES

"Some talk of Alexander, and some of Hercules;
Of Hector and Lysander, and such great names as these;
But of all the world's brave heroes,
there's none that can compare
With a tow, row, row, row, row, row,
for the British Grenadier."
—Anonymous, *The British Grenadier*

Weihsien was a place of heroes; we all knew about Hummel and Tipton and their successful escape, and we all wished we could do the same and become famous. They were certainly the kind of stuff that boys' dreams are made of. But they weren't the only real-life heroes.

A situation like Weihsien is fertile soil for producing people of exceptional character. In our eyes, for instance, our teachers were heroes in the way they absorbed the hardships and fears themselves and tried to make life as normal as possible for us.

In fact, I think at times all of us in camp considered ourselves as heroes. We were surviving, some would say even thriving, in the midst of war. By dint of hard work, ingenuity, faith, prayer and perseverance we had transformed a compound that was a hopeless mess into a habitable and, in some rare corners, almost an attractive living place.

$\mathbb{B}$ut, among many, one hero stands out. Not long after we had moved to Weihsien, another boy and I were playing a game of "conkers" with an acorn suspended on a piece of string. My new-found friend looked up and said, "Do you know who that is coming up the camp road?"

"No," I said as I saw, approaching us with a spring-like walk, a strong, athletic-looking man in baggy shorts down to his knees and a shirt made out of curtain material.

"Why, don't you know? That's Eric Liddell, the Olympic Gold Medalist who wouldn't run on a Sunday."

In that way I first met the athlete who had refused to run in the 100 meters in the 1924 Olympic Games in Paris, but who later won the Gold Medal and created a world record in the 400 meters.[1] Here he was, twenty years later, in his early forties in a prison camp. When he stopped to talk to us, I noticed his friendly smile and the dimple he had on his chin.

I was quite overwhelmed to realize that here in our camp we had this famous sportsman, this brilliant runner. I remember feeling good that even though Eric Liddell wasn't in our mission, he was one of us. He was everybody's hero, but especially ours as he was a missionary. The Edinburgh *Evening News* captured the event that catapulted him to glory back in 1924:

All round the banked area, people were on their feet cheering mad-

[1] Sally Magnusson, *The Flying Scotsman* (London: Quartet Books, 1981).

ly, and as if by magic, hosts of Union Jacks appeared above the heads of the raving crowd as Liddell ripped through the tape and into the arms of the Britishers who were waiting for him. For a moment the cheering lasted, then from the loudspeaker came: "Hello, hello. Winner of the 400 meters: Liddell of Great Britain. The time 47 3/5 is a new world's record." . . . It was the last fifty meters that meant the making or breaking of Liddell. Just for a second it was feared that he would kill himself by the terrible speed he had got up, but to the joy of the British camp, he remained chock full of fight. Imbach, perhaps fifty yards from the tape, fell. It was then Liddell or Fitch. The Scotsman had so surely got all his teeth into the race that the American could not hold, and Liddell got home first.

*H*ow did it come about that Britain's Olympic hero of the 1924 Games was here in Weihsien camp? Eric's parents, James and Mary Liddell, had gone to China from Scotland near the turn of the century as missionaries of the London Missionary Society. Eric's own missionary call had been nurtured at the church of which he was a member, Morningside Congregational Church, and he was a Congregationalist by conviction. He returned to China under the same society as his parents, the London Missionary Society, founded in 1795. David Livingstone had also been a member of LMS.

Eric Liddell's send-off for China was spectacular. Fellow students wheeled him through the streets from Scottish Congregational College at 29 Hope Terrace to Waverley Station in a colorfully decorated carriage. Hundreds jammed the station as the students pulled the carriage right onto the platform, singing as they did so.

Just before getting on the train, Eric was asked to speak. He said he was "Going abroad to endeavor to do his part in trying to unify the countries of the world under Christ," and he expressed the hope that those at home would do their bit. "Let our motto be 'Christ for the World, for the World Needs Christ,'" was his final challenge. Later, standing at the train window, he thrust out his arms to shake the hands stretched out to him, and many were shedding tears. He then led them in singing two verses of the hymn, "Jesus Shall Reign Where'er The Sun."

In China Eric Liddell went to Tientsin, where he joined the staff of the Anglo-Chinese College, a Christian middle school for about five hundred boys. For over ten years he taught science and athletics, his Christian teaching and character deeply influencing the lives of the students. Outside of the College, he took part in a number of athletic meets and gave expert help in the venture of an athletic track in Tientsin.

The most outstanding of Eric Liddell's feats in the early years of his service in China relates more to his dash after an athletic event than to the races themselves. It happened this way: Japan had organized an international sports event in Manchuria in 1928 in connection with the coronation of the Emperor in Japan. Though passed over by the British Olympic Committee for the 1928 Olympics, Eric was invited by the Japanese to compete against the Olympic athletes of France and Japan. At the age of 26, despite limited practice, he was in fine form and easily won the 200 and 400 meters. His boat back to Tientsin was due to leave at 3:00 p.m., and the final race wasn't scheduled until 2:45 p.m. Failing to get the boat's departure delayed, he requested that a taxi with its engine running be waiting for him at the finish line.

As soon as he passed the tape, he kept on running right up to the vehicle. The crowds cheered, and he was just about to leap into the waiting taxi, when the British National Anthem was played, followed straight off by the Marseillaise, forcing him to keep standing at attention as the precious minutes ticked by.

The moment the music stopped he jumped into the taxi, and the vehicle sped off, reaching the wharf in under twenty minutes. By this time the boat was already fifty yards out. But he could see that it would move closer as it rounded the corner of the dock on its way out of the harbor.

Hurdling the dockyard obstructions, he reached the edge of the pier. A wave brought the boat to within fifteen feet, and after quickly throwing his bags on board, Eric took a mighty gazelle-like leap and managed to land at the very back of the moving boat. Those mischief-hiding blue eyes of his had a special twinkle in them the next morning as he stood in front of his class of students and nonchalantly let them into his secret.

*I*n the city of Tientsin he was greatly liked among the missionary community and was often involved in ministry at the Union Church. He became the Sunday school superintendent and had as his pianist Florence McKenzie, the daughter of Mr. and Mrs. Hugh McKenzie, Canadian missionaries working in Tientsin.

Classmates of Florence in the Tientsin International School were John and Bill Toop and their sister Miriam (later Dunn), all three of whom later went back to Asia to serve as missionaries with the Overseas Missionary Fellowship. They have many recollections of humorous incidents and happy picnics associated with Eric. The biggest surprise to all of them—including Florence, since she was ten years his junior—was Eric's proposal of marriage.

Florence, with her lively, outgoing nature, was the perfect complement for Eric, with his more serious and yet fun-loving and spirited outlook. After their engagement Florence returned to Canada, where she took nursing training at Toronto General Hospital, while Eric went home to Scotland for his first furlough. A year later Eric traveled back to China via Canada to see Florence and take some meetings.

In 1934, after Florence had also returned to China, they were married at the Tientsin Union Church. The birth of two daughters, Patricia and Heather, in the years that followed brought great joy to them. But having the two little girls made the decision all the harder when, after much prayer, they agreed that Eric should leave the family temporarily to take up the desperately undermanned evangelistic work in the country.

Going back to Siaochang in southern Hopei, the place where his parents had served for many years, Eric began a life of constant itineration on foot or by bicycle, preaching and teaching, far from the security and relative comfort of the city.

In late 1937 Japan openly invaded China. The nature of the inland work and increasing instability and danger as the Japanese army advanced with reports of widespread barbarism meant it was no place to bring Florence and the girls. Although he would have wished it otherwise, he knew there was no alternative but for them to stay on in Tientsin.

Eric was often caring for very serious physical needs as a result of famine, sickness, or injury. At times he was the lifeline for news and funds for the London Missionary Society staff, working with Dr. Kenneth McAll and the matron, Annie Buchan. To keep them in funds, he used to smuggle currency stuffed in a hollowed-out French bread-roll, which the Japanese soldiers never examined when he had to pass through their blockades. He was always friendly towards the soldiers and managed to distract them from searching him too thoroughly by showing them pictures of his family. Some of the soldiers were moved to tears at the sight of the children and the reminder of their own from whom they were separated.

Eric gives his own account of one incident in the late thirties, when hostilities between the Japanese and Chinese had intensified:

Siaochang Feb. 13th, 1939.

When journeying back from Tientsin to our Mission Station of Siaochang, my colleagues and I heard of a wounded man, lying in a Temple, twenty miles from our Mission Hospital.

No carter would take the risk of taking wounded men, for fear of meeting the Japanese troops on the way. However, one Chinese carter said he would go if I accompanied him. They have a wonderful confidence in us!!! It would be quite dangerous for him, but I think there was no danger as far as I was concerned.

On Saturday, February 18th, the carter started on the journey and some hours later I cycled after him. By evening the carter reached Ho Chu, 18 miles from Siaochang, where we have our Mission premises. I cycled on to Pei Lin Tyu, three miles further on, to see the Headman of the village and make arrangements for the wounded man "to be removed." He lay in the temple about 100 yards outside the village. The temple is a filthy place open to the wind and dust. No one ever comes along to clean it.

No home was open to the wounded man, for if the Japanese descended on them and found that a home had anything to do with the military, it would be destroyed at once, and the lives of those in it would be in danger.

For five days the man had lain in the temple. A friend came daily to the temple to feed the wounded man. He lay on a thin mattress on the ground. When we remember that the nights and days are cold and every night the temperature would be at freezing if not well below it, we marvel that he was still alive.

The Japanese (a tank and ten motor lorries) were at the next village a mile away. I told the wounded man we would be back early the next day and then I returned to Huo Chu. That night, as I lay down, wrapped in my old sheepskin coat, my thoughts turned to the next day. Suppose I met the Japanese, what would I say? I felt for my Chinese New Testament, a book I constantly carried about with me.

It fell open at St. Luke 16. I read until I came to verse 10, and this seemed to me to bring me my answer. "He that is faithful in that which is least is faithful also in much, and he that is unjust in the least is unjust in much." It was as if God had said to me, "Be honest and straight." I turned and went to sleep.

We started early next morning. As we approached the first village, there was a man standing in the entrance to it, beckoning us in. We entered the village and as we passed through it, the Japanese mechanized troops went round it. We fortunately missed each other.

Many of the roads had been dug up, and were like enlarged trenches, and in clambering out our cart overturned.

We reached Pei Lin Tyu early in the day and went to the temple. It was Chinese New Year's Day. People were in the temple burning incense. They were even burning it at the side of the wounded man. I asked the people to come out. I gave them a talk on fresh air being of more value to sick or wounded, than air laden with incense smoke. Then I turned to those great words in Micah "wherewith shall I come before the Lord? Shall I come before Him with burnt offerings—He hath showed Thee, O man, what is good; and what doth the Lord require of Thee but to do justly, and to love mercy, and to walk humbly with Thy God." Sir George Adam Smith in his classic on "The Twelve Minor Prophets," when he comes to this passage writes it in large letters, then says, this is the greatest saying in the Old Testament, and in the New there is only one greater "Come unto Me, all ye that labor and are heavy laden, and I will give you rest." We laid the man in the cart and left.

On reaching Huo Chu, we heard of another wounded man whom we could pick up by going out of our way a short distance. We decided to go and see. When we reached Pang Chuang, we went to see the Headman. He and some others led us to one of the out-houses [shed]. Several men went in first to warn the wounded man that a foreigner was coming in to see him but that he need not be afraid.

On entering I could see, in the dim light a man reclining on a bed; dirty rags were wrapped round his neck. He was one of six men who had been surrounded by the Japanese. They were told to kneel for execution. Five knelt but the sixth remained standing. When the officer came to him, he drew his sword and slashed at him making a gash from the back of his neck round to his mouth. He fell as dead. After the Japanese left, the villagers came out and, finding him still alive, had taken him to this out-house where he had lain for several days.

I told him my cart was only a small one, made for carrying one person, but, that if he was willing to sit on the shafts for 18 miles (5 hours), I would take him to Siaochang Hospital. I could not guarantee his safety if we met the Japanese; he would have to take his chance. He took it. For the first few miles a Japanese aeroplane was circling round slightly south of us. It indicated that the Japanese troops were moving almost parallel to us a mile or two away.

At 4 p.m. we reached the hospital. Two days later the first man died, but the second man lived.

Treated first by Dr. Graham then by Dr. McAll, he soon recovered. His mind turned towards the Christian life and teaching and within a couple of months he made the first steps in Christian living.

In gratitude he painted a number of pictures for me. The one of a peony rose I had lithographed. The saying on it runs "She (the peony) is the most beautiful in the city (China). Her modesty and manner come from God."

As conditions deteriorated in the weeks before the bombing of Pearl Harbor, Eric arranged for his wife and the two children to leave China, planning himself to follow some months later. Safely in Canada, Florence gave birth to their third daughter, Maureen, and the little family waited anxiously for the father's return. But straight after Pearl Harbor Eric was put under house arrest and then in late March 1943, he was among those "enemy nationals" rounded up for internment in Weihsien Civilian Assembly Center, the euphemism for Weihsien Concentration Camp.

Some six months later, when we of the Chefoo Schools arrived at camp, Eric Liddell was already one of the leading influences for good. He was put in one of the dormitories for single men since his family was not with him. As a result of the reshuffle of single men to buildings away from the wall, where they could send signals to the Chinese at nighttime, Eric was moved to the room exactly above where we Prep School boys lived in Block 23. He became warden of our roll-call area.

Eric Liddell was a name that everybody in camp soon got to know. Simply because of his Olympic achievements he was everybody's hero; yet he didn't in any sense rest on his laurels but carried heavy responsibilities and was an outstanding example by his kindness and self-sacrifice. He taught science to the older students, even drawing all the apparatus for chemistry experiments so that the Oxford exams could be taken. He put up a shelf—a valuable item of furniture even if it was only a piece of wood—for a white Russian prostitute in the camp. She said of Eric that he was the only man who ever did anything for her without asking her for favors in return. Often we would see him carrying a heavy load for one of the older people or walking the camp paths with a young person for whom Weihsien imprisonment had brought life to a dead stop. He helped to answer questions and turn the questioning to faith in God and hope that freedom would indeed come someday and with it the chance for education, a profession, marriage and a normal life.

As chairman of the recreation committee, he helped organize the athletic events and worked with our teachers in arranging sports days. I remember him as umpire of our soccer games, which we used to play barefoot on the athletic field by the church. He tore up the sheets he had brought into camp so that he could bind up the field-hockey sticks. In short, he always inspired enthusiasm as he found ways to keep the sports side of camp life going. Strong as he was in his conviction about Sunday not being a day for sports, he even agreed to referee the games of some of the children whose parents let them play on Sundays, when he found them fighting over the game.

To all of us young people in camp, he was known as Uncle Eric. To us he stood out as kind and friendly, with his ever-present smile and gentle, Christ-like manner. He was a true Christian gentleman. He loved children and gave a lot of time to those of us in the Prep School because we were the youngest without our parents. As someone said, he had a Pied-Piper-of-Hamelin quality about him.

Though Eric Liddell missed his family very much, he didn't speak to us very often about them. He wasn't looking for pity. To accept with quiet serenity the will of God was the hallmark of his life. His life was one of a resting faith in the midst of trials, and of these there were many in Weihsien Camp.

Eric ran a Friday-evening youth club, and it was on these occasions as well as the Sunday afternoon services that he loved to speak on such passages as Matthew 5 or 1 Corinthians 13. The manuscript of his devotional book, *A Manual of Christian Discipleship*,[2] was circulated to much profit among quite a number of people in camp.

Camp had the one church building that was fully used all day Sunday, with a Roman Catholic mass first, then an Anglican service, followed by an interdenominational service in the afternoon. At night there was a well-attended hymn sing at which the Salvation Army Band always played.

Many recall the series of messages Eric Liddell gave on the topic of the Holy Spirit. Using a verse a week, he followed the themes in one of his favorite hymns, "Gracious Spirit, Dwell with Me."

> Gracious Spirit, dwell with me—
> I myself would gracious be;
> And with words that help and heal

[2]Eric H. Liddell, *The Disciplines of the Christian Life* (Nashville: Abingdon Press, 1985).

Would Thy life in mine reveal;
And with actions bold and meek
Would for Christ my Savior speak.

Truthful Spirit, dwell with me—
I myself would truthful be;
And with wisdom kind and clear
Let Thy life in mine appear;
And with actions brotherly
Speak my Lord's sincerity.

Tender Spirit, dwell with me—
I myself would tender be;
Shut my heart up like a flower
At temptation's darksome hour;
Open it when shines the sun,
And His love by fragrance own.

Silent Spirit, dwell with me—
I myself would quiet be,
Quiet as the growing blade,
Which through earth its way has made,
Silently, like morning light,
Putting mists and chills to flight.

Mighty Spirit, dwell with me—
I myself would mighty be,
Mighty so as to prevail
Where unaided man must fail:
Ever by a mighty hope
Pressing on and bearing up.

Holy Spirit, dwell with me—
I myself would holy be;
Separate from sin, I would
Choose and cherish all things good,
And whatever I can be
Give to Him who gave me Thee.

—Thomas Toke Lynch

Annie Buchan, who knew Eric well, had been allowed to stay in Peking to care for an elderly patient who was critically ill. When she came into Weihsien in the latter part of 1944 and saw Eric, she could see he had slowed down and that there was something wrong. Only a few weeks before, on one of the sports days, Eric had lost a race. This loss seemed rather puzzling to everyone, as he still looked quite well. However, by December he began to get bad headaches. He spent a while in hospital but then improved and even climbed to the top floor of the hospital to return a plate to someone who had made him something more nourishing. He had to sit down at the top, however, and exclaimed that it was like reaching for the stars. His friends sensed something was seriously wrong. Eric himself wondered if the strain of camp was causing him to break. Everyone knew he had carried a very heavy load physically and emotionally in helping and counseling anyone who needed him.

One wintry day in February, I was with our little group over by the hospital when we saw Eric walking under the trees beside the open space where he had taught us children to play basketball and rounders. As usual he was smiling. As he talked to us, we knew nothing of the pain he was hiding, and he knew nothing of the brain tumor that was to take his life that evening, February 21, 1945, when he, one of the world's greatest athletes, would reach the tape in his final race on earth. He was 43 years old.

Eric Liddell was a man whose strong faith no towering prison walls or barbaric cruelty could conquer. In his last hour he was writing the words of his favorite hymn, and those words brought solace to his soul as they had before when he gave them to the mother whose son had been electrocuted.

Be still, my soul, the Lord is on thy side;

Bear patiently the cross of grief or pain;
Leave to thy God to order and provide;
In every change He faithful will remain.
Be still, my soul, thy best, thy heavenly Friend
Through thorny ways leads to a joyful end.

—Katharina Von Schlegel.

Many times during his last weeks the Salvation Army played this hymn to Sibelius' "Finlandia" outside his window.

The evening snow was falling gently as Eric Liddell died, a soul serene amidst the sorrows and sufferings of the war that was to end six months later. His last words were, "It is complete surrender." His life exemplified the words written in camp by Dr. Hugh Hubbard of the camp committee:

Weihsien—the test—whether a man's happiness depends on what he has or what he is; on outer circumstance, or inner heart; on life's experiences—good and bad—or on what he makes out of the materials those experiences provide.

The shock of Eric Liddell's death rocked the camp. One man who wasn't a Christian, when he heard the news, said, "Yesterday Jesus Christ lived among us; today he is no longer with us." We all missed him.

The Roman Catholic sisters in our building mourned his loss too. He had risked his life some months earlier by going into the morgue to visit Sister Reginald and one of our Chefoo girls, Marjory Windsor, who were both isolated, gravely ill with typhoid fever.

Eric Liddell was buried in the little cemetery in the Japanese part of the camp. Some thirty others who died during internment already had been laid to rest there. Our school was part of the honor guard of children. Very few eyes were dry.

One of the older Chefoo boys was Stephen Metcalf, who today is still serving in Japan after more than thirty years as an

OMF missionary. Just three weeks before Uncle Eric died, he had given Steve his running shoes. Now Steve cherished the gift even more. Though tied together with string and patched with tape, those shoes reminded us all of the true champion Eric Liddell was. Our Olympic hero was a man who was totally committed to putting God first, a man whose humble life combined muscular Christianity with radiant godliness.

Gene Huebener and Joe Cotterill, who roomed with Eric in camp, knew Eric's secret: the unreserved commitment of his life to Jesus Christ as Savior and Lord. That intimacy with God meant everything to him. By the flickering light of a peanut oil lamp early each morning in the men's cramped dormitory, he studied the Bible and talked with God for an hour as he started each day. Evelyn Davey, who was one of our teachers and who met Gene Huebener in camp and married him soon after the war, described Eric Liddell in her diary as "a life poured out for Him in service to others."

It was not until early in May that Florence received in Toronto the letter a friend had typed for Eric on the very day he died. It was still some days later that she and those in Scotland heard the news that he had died.

Beryl Welch (Goodland), aged fourteen, and daughter of one of our Chefoo teachers, wrote in her diary of February 22, 1945: "Dear (Old) Uncle Eric died last night. It was so sudden. He wrote a letter to his wife just that day. Everyone was greatly impressed. I feel so sorry for her. Most people thought he was the best man in the camp. What a loss! It snowed today. There was no coal."

The film *Chariots of Fire* conveys brilliantly the life of a humble man of God, whose athletic prowess brought him fame. We who had the privilege of being with him as he lived and suffered his last years caught a glimpse of the depth of his love for God and His Word that enabled him to walk away from the glory this world offered in exchange for a glory that surpasses everything in time and eternity.

Destined for Glory

(To the tune of *Chariots of Fire* theme)

We're destined for glory, far brighter than gold
In the race of a lifetime, swift, eager and bold.
Both eyes fixed on Jesus, His joy our desire;
Strong feet run to follow, like chariots of fire.
His pleasure's worth more than wealth and fame
His truth above all
To hear God's "Well done," and praise His name,
Our soul's highest goal.

We're destined for glory, far brighter than gold
In the race of a lifetime, swift, eager and bold.
Both eyes fixed on Jesus, His joy our desire;
Strong feet run to follow, like chariots of fire.

—David Michell

Chapter 9

LIKE SAVIORS FROM ANOTHER WORLD

"O happy band of pilgrims
Look upward to the skies . . ."
—James Neale, *Hymns of the Eastern Church*

In the bitter winter of 1945, food was becoming more scarce and our clothes reaching the point of being more "skinbare" than threadbare. We had the feeling that Christina Rossetti's Christmas Carol would have been a good choice for the camp theme song:

In the bleak mid winter
Frosty wind made moan,
Earth stood hard as iron,
Water like a stone;
Snow had fallen, snow on snow,
Snow on snow
In the bleak mid winter,
Long ago.

The strain of prison-camp life was telling on many people.

There were signs of this too among the Japanese. While they didn't say anything publicly, we were beginning to sense that the tide of the war was turning against them. The belligerence and arrogance of some showed itself more fiercely, while others made guarded overtures, perhaps subconsciously wanting to save their necks. We really didn't know how to interpret their behavior.

Rumors were rife, in fact, that in the event of defeat, the Japanese had orders never to surrender but to first kill all prisoners and then themselves. Hummel and Tipton, still in hiding with the Nationalist soldiers about thirty miles from Weihsien on the Shantung Peninsula, had even more cause to be alarmed than we had. Over their radio they picked up news that at the time of the American landing in the Philippines, the Japanese had massacred Catholic Fathers and civilians. This was one time we were glad that not all the news reached us.

"Man's extremity is God's opportunity" was amply illustrated in Weihsien. While there were those who cursed God and saw the whole of their camp existence as a hell-sized hiatus in their lives, there were others who said, "I thank God for Weihsien Camp," and "I came to know a lot more about myself and other people." Some could even say, "I came to know Christ in Weihsien Camp."

As there were not a few similarities in our camp experience to the Israelites' journeyings in the wilderness and their imprisonment in exile, Israel's struggles and trials formed the basis of many a message or Bible study. The Word of the Lord through the whole Old Testament historical record, particularly the Psalms, brought comfort and hope through the long months and years of prolonged isolation. Time without number we sang together what became our internment hymn, "God is our refuge and our strength" (Psalm 46).

As war dragged on, the Japanese invasion of China overtook many of our parents who were in the path of their juggernaut advance. To witness the horror of the soldiers' brutality as they tortured, raped, and killed was a great trauma. Leaving their fellow church workers and the beleaguered flock of believers in such times was indeed a painful experience for all missionaries. Yet as Japanese bombs fell, they were forced to flee, escaping with their lives but almost nothing else.

It was in conditions such as these that my parents with my younger sister and brother made their way out of China and traveled via India to Australia during the latter part of the war. How hard it must have been for them and many other parents to leave some of their children behind while the war was still raging!

In some of the more remote parts of China, the Japanese had not been able to gain control, but infiltration was going on all the time. The common pattern replicated in many parts of China was of conflict between the Nationalists, the communists, the Japanese, and the local guerilla or bandit groups.

John and Edith Bell from Canada, who were in pioneer work in Kansu (Gansu) province in the far northwest, had sent three of their children to Chefoo School, and it had been years since they had seen them, and months since the last Red Cross letter from Weihsien had gotten through. Edith, like all other missionary mothers bereft of their children, longed and prayed for the day when she would see them again. Edith tells what it was like for her:

> During the war many people came up to northwest China, and as the communists had crept in, we didn't know whether we were entertaining friend or foe. There was one man who brought us news about our children. He was a well educated man, and one evening he came to visit. He came from eastern China, and it was the first time that

he had traveled as far west. We received so little news of the children, and even when the Red Cross letters came, we often couldn't decipher the words because stamped on top of it was Prisoner of War.

This Chinese young man talked for a long time about his experiences whenever he came to see us, and he seemed to know details of the children being in the Weihsien Camp. He told us they were well cared for with enough food and clothing, and it was certainly like water to a thirsty soul to get even a few words of news.

Just a few days before Christmas he came when I was at home alone. He talked for a long time that evening and then said, "Mrs. Bell, I have some very sad news to tell you."

"Oh," I replied, "and we're so happy because we are celebrating the Lord Jesus' birthday."

He hedged for a while, and then finally he said, "All the students in the Weihsien Camp have been murdered."

Well, I held my breath for a wee while, and then I picked up my Bible, and I turned to Jeremiah 31, verses 16 and 17. This was the verse that God had given to me not long after my children were interned: "Refrain thy voice from weeping and thine eyes from tears, saith the Lord. Your work will be rewarded. Your children will come from the land of the enemy, and they will come to their own border." Well, I showed him my Chinese Bible. I said, "Doctor (he was not a medical doctor), you read this." He read it and threw my Bible on the table in anger. Then I knew he was not my friend.

Before he stomped out of the house, I pled with him: "Please don't go over to Dr. Hoyte's house and say this to him."

However, without any consideration at all, the man went straight over to Dr. Hoyte, who was at the Borden Memorial Hospital. Stanley Hoyte had already suffered greatly. His wife Grace, (the daughter of Robert P. Wilder, famous in the Student Volunteer Movement) had died during the war while their five children were away at Chefoo school and also interned in Weihsien Camp.

I couldn't stop the man's going, and he burst into Dr. Hoyte's room and told him the same bad news. The news was almost too much for Dr. Hoyte, and some of the other men had to come and help him. By this time I was close enough to be able to call out that the man was an imposter, and I held up my Bible with God's promise to me from Jeremiah.

Back in Weihsien camp the second week of August was very busy for our coolie couriers. They brought in news from Tipton and Hummel that there were signs of surrender. The rumor factory in camp was never busier, but August 15, VJ Day, came and went just like any other day, with no definite news from our camp leaders or the Japanese.

Friday, August 17, started ordinarily enough. The work squads were going about their usual duties in the kitchens, at the ash heaps, or other places. When at 9:00 a.m. our class went down to the church for our weekly singing lesson, little did we know we were coming up to one of those moments whose every detail would be etched on our memories.

The mid-summer sun seemed to be beckoning us as it filtered through the ornate corner windows of the church. "Let's try it one more time," our singing teacher said, with a hint of resignation. I was trying hard to hit the high notes but the weekly spoonful of crushed eggshells (for calcium), coaxed down my throat by the teacher that morning, turned my efforts into a sound little better than a growl.

We were droning our best, when all at once everything was drowned out by a deafening roar right over our heads. Above the din we heard frantic shouts of "American plane! American plane! It's heading straight for us." We dashed outside and were caught in a frenzied flow of able-bodied inmates pouring out of the little shacks and crowded rooms onto the athletic field. The pumps, the coal balls, the washing and even the kitchens were abandoned. We all ran to join the swelling throng already gazing raptly skyward, hearts pounding uncontrollably. Could it be that at last our three years of captivity were about to end?

The plane had turned and was coming in very low, just sweeping over the lookout towers and the walls. Shirts and arms were waving wildly as people began to jump up and down. Hysteria was at fever pitch, with some running in panic to and fro, others frozen to the ground, their upturned faces and searching eyes magnetized as it were by the huge B-24. As the plane came down lower, we could see people inside and then its name, "The Armored Angel."

The plane flew right over, and we expected that any moment the Japanese soldiers would open fire on it. Then slowly, slowly the plane started upward again, moving away from the camp. Was it going to leave us after all? Then, to the piercing shrieks and wild cries of everyone, seven GI's parachuted down, floating out of the sky like saviors from another world.

Nothing could stop us now. The forbidding gray walls and massive gates in an instant lost their terror. Not even the guards with their bayonets drawn as they stood in line could block our headlong stampede. Some of us children, barefoot and dressed only in shorts, were first down the cinder road to the main gate. We hesitated only momentarily as we neared the soldiers. The shouts and cheers behind us and the hope of deliverance within reach took away our fears. As we surged through the gates with spirits bursting for freedom from the years of imprisonment, the guards fell away to the sides.

The stronger men, who reached the Americans first, were met by drawn pistols, since the GIs were prepared to meet Japanese soldiers. Henry Lack, one of our Chefoo boys, wearing only shorts and covered with soot from head to foot from stoking, came upon one of the airmen. Challenged the GI: "Are you British or American?"

Flustered by the pistol, young Henry apologized for his blackened appearance and said, "I'm *supposed* to be British!"

Stowing away his pistol, the GI responded, "Boy, good to meet you; the war is over, and we'll soon have you out of this."

Another of the GIs was seized by one of the women, who hugged him around the neck and kissed him before fainting in his arms. Not so amorously inclined, the airman yelled to his buddies, "Hey, you guys, take this dame off my neck!"

In no time the parachutists were hoisted up by the prisoners onto the men's shoulders above the head-height corn and tall sorghum stalks, besieged by adoring girls and wide-eyed children. One GI's remark was long remembered: "I wouldn't change places with Clark Gable for all the tea in China."

We younger children couldn't get there fast enough to be part of the first welcome. Though the soles of our feet were hardened from the barefoot life, our camp had long since been denuded of every prickle, and now the prickles on the dirt road slowed us down.

As a small group of us were limping along, eyes strained in the direction of where the parachutes had disappeared, we suddenly heard screams warning us to look out. A bundle without a parachute had been thrown out of the plane and was hurtling towards us. Like pillars of salt we stopped dead in our tracks. The bundle kept plunging earthward and then with a terrifying impact buried a Chinese farmer in the field and bounced over our heads, showering us with dust and stones before landing in a little muddy creek that ran through the village.

The farmer was dug out and carried into camp. After being unconscious for two weeks, he recovered and was given reparation for his injuries. This near tragedy for us was quickly forgotten as the triumphant procession of shoulder-borne liberators approached. We tagged along, shouting and cheering as we tugged the billowing folds of parachutes along the ground, bringing up the rear. What a triumphal procession we were! No ticker-tape parade could ever have matched it.

Main Street by now was packed with people. Nobody could stand to miss anything. The camp band was ready for this day and had taken up their positions at the back of the church. As the procession came nearer, they struck up the medley which they had in readiness. We had always loved to watch the band practice. Even the Japanese guards had often stood and listened. But neither they nor we had caught on to their scheme. Little did we realize that the cleverly disguised drills that we had been listening to over the past months were various national anthems without the melody! Now loud and clear the notes rang out above the din, and Americans, British, Chinese, and others joined in singing the songs of victory.

As we neared the gates, tension grew. But nothing happened. Exuberant spirits won the day as we pressed into the camp, where pandemonium had broken loose. The leader of the parachutists, Major Stanley Staiger, from Klamath Falls, Oregon, pushed through the crowd into the guardhouse with both pistols drawn to confront the commandant, who must have known the war was over because he and the whole garrison surrendered without resistance.

In a master stroke of face-saving, the Americans handed back the role of security of the camp to the Japanese. After all, what could seven GIs do? They hadn't even come to take over! Our new heroes, Major Staiger and his men, explained that they had really come only to assess the situation and make arrangements to evacuate the critically ill and the elderly.

One of the team, of whom we were particularly proud, was Navy Lieutenant Jimmy Moore, a graduate of Chefoo School. He was the son of missionaries and had volunteered to be in the first reconnoiter party because many of us were missionaries and children. When he reached the camp, his first words were, "Take me to Mr. Bruce!"

Some years later, General Wedemeyer, who had been in charge of the rescue of foreign prisoners in China, said that in his view the rescue attempt by the seven was a "suicide mission" because of the paranoid military intentions of Japan to kill all Allied captives.

Sunday, August 19 was set apart for thanksgiving services. Tears flowed and hearts overflowed with gratitude to God that the end had come at last and in a manner that had given us such a powerful object lesson that the meek shall inherit the earth.

At the service, everyone who had any kind of uniform wore it. We put on our Cub outfits and the girls their faded Brownie dresses. The Guides, Scouts, Rangers, the ex-servicemen, and Salvation Army officers too all dressed up for the occasion in the remnants of their uniforms.

Our liberators set things in motion for those needing immediate medical help to be shipped out. Wherever the GIs walked, a procession of admirers followed behind them, and I'm sure they must have enjoyed it.

On August 20, many more American soldiers under their leader, Colonel Hyman Weinburg, arrived by truck at the front gate. They had been flown in to a makeshift airfield five miles from camp and, after they arrived, took over from the Japanese, who laid down their rifles, bowed their heads, and then quietly melted away to join their garrison in retreat.

Weihsien. Sept. 6. 1945.

To: Internees, Weihsien Civilian Assembly Centre.

In anticipation at the departure from this area of the undersigned officers and enlisted men of the United States Armed Forces, it is our desire and wish that this letter be brought to the attention of all internees.

The sincere manifestations of good-will, appreciation of our work and in particular the efforts of the Camp Committee and all concerned in the whole-hearted support of our team, facilitated our task immeasurably.

We want each of you to know that any success achieved in the performance of our duties, from the moment of our arrival to the completion of our mission, is largely due to the excellent administrative organisation already in existence and the complete co-operation so freely and cheerfully displayed by all on our behalf.

We feel that the attitude of the internees is indicative of the true ideals that made possible the total victory of all Allied Forces during the titanic war now successfully concluded

Further the conduct and adaption of you towards the difficult and trying circumstances of the three unfortunate years now passed, merits our most sincere respect and profound admiration.

Stanley. A. Staiger,
Major— U.S Army.

Willis. S. Georgia.
Captain.— U.S. Army.

J. Walton. Moore.
Lt — United States Navy.

James. J. Hannon.
Lt. U.S. Army.

Tadashi. T. Nagaki.
Sgt.— U.S. Army.

Ray. N. Hanchulak.
Sgt.— U.S. Army.

Peter. C. Orlich.
Cpl. — U.S. Army.

Mr. Cheng. Han. Wang.
Interpreter.

The hand-printed letter of appreciation the seven airmen and their interpreter wrote to the Weihsien internees.

The American military told us about the atom bomb and how the war ended. Orientation classes were started, magazines distributed and a library set up, all for the purpose of paving the way for our much anticipated departure.

Orientation took some getting used to. The overzealous efforts of the recreation officer produced "Oh What a Beautiful Morning!" sung by Gordon McCrae—or was it Frank Sinatra? However, when this came blaring out at six o'clock in the morning over the rigged-up loudspeaker system, there was not much appreciation for the rude awakening. What the well-meaning officer thought would be just what everybody wanted turned out to be the last thing people needed. One man, obviously not an American, with no attempt at subtlety, snipped the wire, plunging the camp back into its accustomed quiet. He was heard to mutter, "We need the war back again in order to get peace!"

*T*he kind of peace and quiet—"tedium" might be a better word—we had known at times before was gone forever. Within a few days planes were sighted on the horizon, and very soon eleven Super Fortresses from Guam were just outside the camp raining down forty-four gallon drums filled with canned fruit. Even with two parachutes the drums were too heavy, and they plummeted down like bombs, exploding and sinking half buried into the ground. When the all-clear was given, we rushed out and drank down Del Monte peaches by the tin full.

A local farmer, who was not much more than skin and bone, did not fare quite as well. As the canned fruit "bombs" dropped on and around his village, he was not able to get out of the way in time. Though he jumped back at the last minute, his big toe was chopped off by a drum as it hit the earth. The impact threw him backwards, and he disappeared from sight down a well. He was quickly rescued, however, and brought into camp for treatment.

After a few more days had passed, scores of five-carton packages of food, clothing, confectionaries, and medicines replaced the drums, and these were carried in by willing hands for distribution. What a sight it was to see a floating rainbow of parachutes across the sky! The heavens literally opened with blessings we will never forget.

Strangely, there was one parachute drop some people in the camp wished they could forget. The words DROP HERE had been made out of silk from the parachutes and laid out in a big field in front of the camp. Most of the drops were successfully made in that general area. However, one of the planes misfired, and this is how it happened: parachutes were in such abundant supply that we kids not only made a new game out of taking jumps from the mountain of piled-up parachutes, but we used the brightly colored chutes to decorate the playing field for a sports day in honor of the occasion. One pilot brought his B-29 right above us and gave the order, "Bomb racks open!" Underdoors parted, and boxes came crashing down onto the camp.

We kids loved it, but I saw one older lady, close to a nervous wreck at the best of times, look up in panic as she saw a parachute chasing her. She took off into the air as if she was going to meet the parachute halfway, but was saved the effort as a tree checked its fall. She crumpled up on the ground exhausted, with the parachute's great silk panels gently enfolding her.

After the planes had dropped their supplies, we gathered what we could and brought them into the church, where they were sorted. We had never seen a warehouse sale or any kind of sale for that matter, but the church resembled one at that moment. One lineup about which there were no complaints for a change

レンゴウグンホリョヘ

ALLIED PRISONERS

The JAPANESE Government has surrendered. You will be evacuated by ALLIED NA-
TIONS forces as soon as possible.

Until that time your present supplies will be augmented by air-drop of U.S.
food, clothing and medicines. The first drop of these items will arrive within one
(1) or two (2) hours.

Clothing will be dropped in standard packs for units of 50 or 500 men. Bundle
markings, contents and allowances per man are as follows:

BUNDLE MARKINGS

50 MAN PACK	500 MAN PACK	CONTENTS	ALLOWANCES PER MAN
A	3	Drawers	
A	1-2	Undershirt	2
B	22	Socks (pr)	2
A	4-6	Shirt	2
A	7-9	Trousers	1
C	23-30	Jacket, field	1
A	10	Belt, web, waist	1
A	11	Capt, H.B.T.	1
B	12-21	Shoes (pr)	1
A	1-2	Handkerchiefs	3
C	32-34	Towel	1

BUNDLE MARKINGS

50 MAN PACK	500 MAN PACK	CONTENTS	ALLOWANCES PER MAN
B	10	Laces, shoe	1
A	11	Kit, sewing	1
C	31	Soap, toilet	1
C	4-6	Razor	1
C	4-6	Blades, razor	1
B	10	Brush, tooth	10
C	31	Paste, tooth	1
B	10	Comb	1
C	32	Shaving cream	1
C	12-21	Powder(insecticide)	1

There will be instructions with the food and medicine for their use and distribution.

DO NOT OVEREAT OR OVERMEDICATE   C A U T I O N   FOLLOW DIRECTIONS

INSTRUCTIONS FOR FEEDING 100 MEN

To feed 100 men for the first three (3) days, the following blocks (individual
bundles dropped) will be assembled:

3 Blocks No. 1
(Each Contains)

2 Cases, Soup, Can
1 Cases Fruit Juice
1 Case Accessory Pack

1 Block No. 5
(Each Contains)

1 Case Soup, Dehd
1 Case Veg Puree
1 Case Bouillon
1 Case Hosp Supplies
1 Case Vitamin Tablets

1 Block No. 3
(Each Contains)

1 Case Candy
1 Case Gum
1 Case Cigare
1 Case Matche

3 Blocks No. 2
(Each Contains)

3 Cases "C" Rations
1 Case Hosp Supplies
2 Cases Fruit

1 Block No. 7
(Each Contains)

1 Case Nescafe
1 Sack Sugar
1 Case Milk
1 Case Cocoa

1 Block No. 10
(Each Contains)

3 Cases Fruit
2 Cases Juice

One of the
leaflets
dropped from
B29s
to Weihsien
prisoners.

was the one for the distribution. My portion for August 29 was two towels, three handkerchiefs, one cap, four tins of food (one was "chopped pork and egg yolks"), two big and four small chocolate bars, ten packets of chewing gum—Chiclets and Beechnut were two I remember—and ten boxes of cigarettes! We bartered well with the latter.

Much of the food was completely new to us. I recall having no idea what ketchup was. I found it a bit thick to drink but loved it. Likewise with the Chiclets. Though hard to swallow, I kept getting them down and popping in another delicious-tasting white square until somebody told me, "You don't eat them; you just keep on chewing!"

We devoured so much chocolate we couldn't even look at it after a few days. Gone forever were our desserts of acacia flowers stripped from the trees. Though our stomachs were in turmoil, who could be ill at such a time? We heard of some people in the camp hospital who, when they heard the GIs had landed, jumped out of bed and out of the windows, never to return.

Freedom had come at last. Weihsien Concentration Camp was almost history. Now we had to get *home!*

Chapter 10

FROM THE LAND OF THE ENEMY

"Refrain thy voice from weeping and thine eyes from tears.
Your work will be rewarded.
Your children will come from the land of the enemy,
and they will come to their own border"

—God's promise to Edith Bell
from Jeremiah 31:16–17.

By the last week of September everything was settled for us to leave. We kids were excited and impatient. Older folk and the infirm were to go first. One of the earliest to be repatriated was white-bearded Herbert Taylor, known to all of us as Grandpa Taylor. Though a bit more bent over at the age of 85, he had not only withstood the rigors of internment, but his blue eyes and his faith were bright and undiminished.

Our impatience was more than matched by that of parents waiting for us either in far-off parts of China or further off in homelands. They had perhaps suffered the most in the years of separation. The mother of four of Grandpa Taylor's grandchildren who were also with us at Weihsien, Alice Taylor, described the agony, faith, and final ectasy of those years in an unforgettable way for readers of *Guideposts* Magazine:

> I sent frequent letters to Chefoo, telling the children where we were, and somehow, miraculously, a few letters came to us from the children. They'd had Sunday dinner with Grandpa. Kathleen, fourteen, had earned another Girl Guides badge. Jamie, ten, had breezed through his exams. Mary had just celebrated her ninth birthday. John, eight, had been sick, but was much better. And, briefly, there had been some ground skirmishes between Japanese troops and Chinese guerillas, but the school had escaped harm, and the fighting had subsided.
>
> I would take out the children's letters and re-read them until they became frayed at the edges. I agonized over the lack of news. "James," I would say, "do you think the children are all right? It's been so long since we've heard anything." With his quiet faith James reassured me. But I saw the worry in his eyes. And I knew that his very human fear for the children's safety was just as great as mine.
>
> I pictured them over and over—the times we spent together reading and talking and singing around the organ. I remembered them the way they looked the day James and I left Chefoo—Kathleen in a navy-blue jumper and white blouse, her long, wavy hair falling past her shoulders; Mary with her blond bob and pretty blue eyes; our sons, young and full of promise.
>
> "Heavenly Father, keep them safe," I prayed. "Watch over Grandpa Taylor." The air raids sent us running for shelter day after day. Epidemics raged among the Chinese soldiers. In parts of China food was so scarce because of drought that people were eating tree bark. In the midst of this—with missionaries helping with relief programs, passing out food and clothes to refugees—James and I started the Northwest Bible Institute to prepare young people for the ministry. Somehow, we knew, God's work had to go on, and we spent long hours developing a curriculum and preparing teachers, then enrolling students.
>
> One day, after teaching a class, I was just entering our house when the newspaper deliveryman came. The paper's large Chinese characters announced: "Pearl Harbor Attacked. U.S. Enters War." As I ab-

sorbed the news, I realized why there had been a long silence from the children. Chefoo had been in the Japanese line of attack.

"Oh, dear God," I whispered, "my children, my children . . . ." I knelt beside the bed. Not even tears came at first, just wave after wave of anguish.

As the fear penetrated deeper, I remembered the horror stories of Nanking—where all of the young women of that town had been brutally raped. And I thought of our lovely Kathleen, beginning to blossom into womanhood . . . .

Great gulping sobs wrenched my whole body. I lay there, gripped by the stories we had heard from refugees—violent deaths, starvation, the conscription of young boys—children—to fight.

I thought of ten-year-old Jamie, so conscientious, so even-tempered. "What has happened to Jamie, Lord? Has someone put a gun in his hands? Ordered him to the front lines? To death?" Mary and John, so small and so helpless, had always been inseparable. "Merciful God," I cried, "are they even alive?"

Kneeling there by the bed, pleading with God, I knew without any doubt at all that I had no other hope but God. I reached out to Him now, completely. "Please help my children. Let them be alive, please!" Then, as if in a dream, I drifted back to a time when I was a girl of sixteen in Wilkes-Barre, Pennsylvania. I pictured our minister, Pa Ferguson, sitting there telling me words he had spoken years ago. "Alice, if you take care of the things that are dear to God, He will take care of the things dear to you." That was Pa Ferguson's translation of "Seek ye first the kingdom of God, and His righteousness; and all these things shall be added unto you" (Matt. 6:33). It was his way of making his point to the teenagers he was working with.

In the stillness of the bedroom I pondered Pa Ferguson's words. Who were the ones dear to God? The Chinese to whom God had called me to minister. And who were the ones dear to me? My children.

I did not know whether my children were dead or alive; nevertheless a deep peace replaced my agony. This war had not changed God's promise. With that assurance I felt the aching weight of fear in my stomach lift.

"All right, God," I said finally, "John and Mary and Kathleen and Jamie are in Your care. With all my heart I believe that You will guard them. I know that You will bring us back together, and until that day comes, I will put all my energy into Your work. I promise." We had a pact, God and I, and I knew He would keep His part of it. And I must keep mine.

So it went each day—taking care of the things dear to God: Like the day at the house of Mr. Chang, whose body and mind were devastated by disease. "He will not let anyone near the house," his wife warned.

I walked to the window and called: "Mr. Chang, we have come to pray for you. You can be healed. Please let us come in." And he did! He turned his life over to God. And I knew that God was watching over my children.

There were times when I rode into the hills with our new baby, Bertie, strapped on my back and held open-air meetings with people in remote villages. "This is for You, Heavenly Father," I would say in prayer, "because these are Your children, dear to You." And I knew that He was caring for my children too.

And in the compound, when I worked as a mid-wife delivering babies, I would say to God, "Thank You for letting me deliver this child." And I thanked Him for delivering my children from harm.

In time we received word that everyone in Chefoo School had been captured and crammed into a concentration camp in Weihsien along with 1,300 other captives. But we had no way of knowing, from day to day, whether the children were alive.

People would say to me, "You have such great strength, Alice, carrying on, yet knowing that your children have been captured." And I would say, "My strength is God's strength. I know He will not forsake my children. I know this." Through it all—the scarcity, the sickness, the dying, through the bombings when I didn't breathe until I heard the explosions and realized I was still alive—I did what I knew God wanted me to do. I took care of the Chinese. I passed along His Word to doctors, to army officers and troops, to students, to parents and grandparents. Over and over, day after day.

In spare moments after school I began sewing clothes for Kathleen and Mary. "What is that you're making, wifey?" James asked, using his usual term of endearment.

"Some pajamas for the girls, James, for when they come back. I hope I've judged the sizes right." He was silent. Just looked at me.

Then one Sunday morning, as I held services in a village twenty miles from Genghsiang, one of the students from the Bible institute appeared in the crowd, pushing my bicycle, and announced, "They say that the Japanese have surrendered." The crowd burst into excitement. But for days confusion reigned. Families had been torn apart, homes demolished, records lost or burned. Communication and transportation were haphazard.

I longed to hear some word, just to know. . . . And as I sat one September evening in our home during a faculty meeting, my mind wandered once more to the children. Again I pictured them as I had seen them last, waving goodbye. I heard their voices, faintly, calling excitedly. Then I heard their voices louder. Was I imagining this? No, their voices were real! And they came bursting through the doorway. "Mommy, Daddy, we're home—we're home!" And they flew into our arms. Our hugs, our shouts filled the room. We couldn't let go of one another. It had been five and a half long, grueling years. Yet there they were—thin, but alive and whole, laughing and crying. Oh, they had grown! But Kathleen still wore the same blue jumper she had worn when I last saw her. It was as though God had miraculously preserved the children and returned them to us.

Later medical checkups showed their health to be excellent. There were no emotional repercussions, and when we went to the States a year later, our children were two years ahead of students their own age.

While many in Japanese concentration camps suffered horrors, the children of the Chefoo School were spared. They received dedicated care from their teachers, and when there was not enough food to go around, the teachers helped the children to gather wild edible plants. The children continued their lessons, and they attended church. Jamie looked after Grandpa Taylor, who was flown back to England after the war. And today Jamie—James Hudson Taylor III—works with Overseas Missionary Fellowship (the continuation of the China Inland Mission) [as General Director] in Singapore. For our family that advice from Pa Ferguson long years ago will always hold special meaning. I pass it along to you, for it is truly so: "If you take care of the things that are dear to God, He will take care of the things dear to you."[1]

We heard that the day for our departure would be September 24. As the day approached, I couldn't help feeling a bit sad at leaving. We had come to know the camp so well. It had been home to us for a long time. But when the 24th dawned, our excitement was dampened only slightly by rain coming down in torrents.

The day that we had dreamed about for years, however, was to bring heartbreaking disappointment. Though our party of missionaries and children were loaded up into the trucks, the rain had turned the roads into quagmires, and we had to turn back.

The next day went better, and on September 25 580 of us rumbled out on trucks through the camp gates and bounced our way to Weihsien city, where we boarded the train. We rolled out of Weihsien toward the coast not a day too soon, as guerillas blew up the track the very next morning.

What a royal welcome the Chinese people of Tsingtao gave us! As the train chugged into this coastal city, crowds lined the streets with banners held high, announcing "Grateful Welcome to Our Allies."

In the crowd that day was a Christian lady who had been an *amah* for many years at the Girls' School in Chefoo. She had wept as she watched us being marched off into concentration camp three years before. Now, with tears of joy streaming

---

[1] Alice Hayes Taylor, "He Will Not Forsake My Children." Reprinted by permission by *Guideposts* Magazine. Copyright © 1983 by Guideposts Associates, Inc., Carmel, New York 10512.

down her cheeks, she met staff and students again. She said, "I had often seen big ones going away, but never all those little ones. I have prayed for you every day, and now, surely, it is the Lord's grace to bring you out this way so that I can see how my prayers have been answered. My heart is satisfied."

At a special celebration, the mayor of Tsingtao presented each one of us with a beautiful silk handkerchief. We all stayed at the city's finest hotel—Edgewater Mansions. The British cruiser H.M.S. *Bermuda* feted us to a party on deck.

But freedom was surprisingly hard to handle. We didn't know how to cope with running water, money, stores, new sights and open spaces. Our eyes were dazzled. We had our first swim, and as one of the teachers remarked, "We looked clean for the first time in years." That was at least a better response than the little boy whose memories knew nothing before Weihsien. When he saw the sea for the first time he said, "Mommy, look at that great big cesspool!"

The Chinese Christian community invited us to a united thanksgiving service in one of their churches. The fellowship with Chinese Christians, which had been reluctantly broken because of the war, was joyfully renewed. Gratitude and hilarity marked the occasion as several of our missionaries spoke on life in camp. We could laugh about it now. The Chinese Christians provided special music, one being an item from a four-year-old girl playing beautifully on the piano.

Within two weeks the American forces made arrangements for most of us to travel down the coast on the U.S.S. *Geneva*, a troop ship that had been prepared for the invasion of Japan. We left on October the 7th, my 12th birthday, most of which I spent sitting on the dock with a fever of 103° F. Though battered in the tail end of a typhoon, we reached Hong Kong safely.

*I*n Hong Kong the British RAPWI (Repatriation of Allied Prisoners of War and Internees) cared for us. Soliders treated us royally, taking us for cruises in their jeeps and trucks. And the British Red Cross put on teas and picnics for us, with all kinds of goodies.

Hearing in Hong Kong about the terrible conditions in the concentration camp at local Camp Stanley, we came to realize how much we had to be thankful for at Weihsien. As children we would never have survived what the prisoners faced under the Japanese military at Stanley.

Swarms of captured Japanese soldiers were being marched around in our area. A squad of them, in fact, were ordered to carry our baggage.

Close by the army camp was a mountain of swords and gas masks taken from the surrendered soldiers. *What loot!* we thought, with envious looks. Despite the security, I managed to "scrounge" some .303 bullets and gas-mask sprays. Habit was dying hard.

My mischievous behavior didn't end there either. Behind the Argyle Street apartments, where we were staying, were some low hills. Hills, like the sea, had been completely outside our experience during the last three years in camp. Deciding to go for a climb one afternoon, four of us boys started up a ravine. This ascent being too slow for me, I branched off on my own, climbing onto a ridge which I was sure would get me to the top faster. I lost the others from view but kept pressing on up the sharp grade. All of a sudden I lost my nerve—above me it was too steep to go further, while beside and below me the mountain face was brittle and crumbling. I couldn't move. Directly below I could see a drop of a hundred feet or more.

In desperation I called out to my friends, but there was no response. *After all these years, how could God let me die like this?* my heart wailed. Then I cried to Him to help me: "O God, You've done so much for us. Your promises are just the same. Please help me. I want to serve You with my life." God did help me. I calmed down and after a few minutes began to inch back the way I had come. After what seemed like hours I reached level ground again.

> "O Jesus, I have promised
> To serve Thee to the end;
> Be Thou forever near me,
> My Master and my Friend!
> I shall not fear the battle,
> If Thou art by my side;
> Nor wander from the pathway,
> If Thou wilt be my Guide.
>
> O Jesus, Thou hast promised
> To all who follow Thee,
> That where Thou art in glory
> There shall Thy servant be!
> And, Jesus, I have promised
> To serve Thee to the end,
> Oh, give me grace to follow,
> My Master and my Friend."
>
> **—John E. Bode**

As the complex task went on of making travel arrangements from Hong Kong to many parts of the world for all who had been released from prison camps, the British troops continued to give us the thrill of our lives as they took us in their jeeps to many places of interest. I was the thirteenth one day to squeeze into one jeep on its way to the airport. Was I ever glad I got on, as we were shown over a number of the planes and were enraptured watching the planes take off and land.

But waiting for a berth home also meant that we had the privilege of hearing Lutheran Pastor Kiyoshi Watanabe speak.

While other Japanese were now in camps in the city, this man was free in recognition of his service to prisoners during the war. At great risk to himself, he had funneled medicine, letters, food, and the like to prisoners at both Stanley and Shamshuipo Camps. Ironically he later returned to Japan to discover that his home and family, except for one daughter, had been wiped out by the atomic bomb at Hiroshima.

During the weeks following our release, communication was restored with the outside world. With overwhelming relief parents scattered around the world received word of the safety of their children. Dorothy Bell of Toronto writes of the experience for her and her husband, George:

> One September day I was on my knees scrubbing the kitchen floor when a neighbor called to say we were wanted on the telephone. We had placed an order for a phone more than a year earlier but it had not been installed. George ran next door as I was not very presentable. In a moment he was back with word that the children had been released. The Toronto *Star* had called to let us know. We turned on the radio and heard the announcement: "The following Canadians have been released from Japanese internment camps: Agnes Bell, Edith Bell, George Bell, Kenneth Bell, Ruth Bell . . . "—three of ours and two of the John Bell's children! We laughed, we cried, we praised the Lord. I don't remember whether I ever did finish washing that kitchen floor. We called one or two relatives and asked them to pass along the news. For us at last the war was over. The children were safe and would soon be on the way home.[2]

The Canadian party, including the Bell children, left on the *Samstrule,* a steamer built to carry water and freight. The ship steamed out of Hong Kong December 3 and dropped anchor

[2]Dorothy Bell, *Nannie's Story: In Weakness, Strength* (Coburg, Ontario: privately published, 1979).

off Saanichton Bay near Victoria, British Columbia, Christmas Day.

And what a day it was! The Soldiers' and Airmen's Christian Association got permission to get the party all off so they could enjoy Christmas dinner and Christian hospitality on shore. At the CIM home in Vancouver, after a brief rest, kids and escorts enjoyed a specially saved Christmas dinner, followed by a time of praise and thanksgiving to God for their safe return.

On January the 9th the remnant of the party were welcomed at Toronto train station by teary-eyed parents, other CIM missionaries, and friends.

But missing at the train station were parents John and Edith Bell. Still on their own way home from China, they were steaming toward New York Harbor. Edith Bell tells her story:

> For the last months of the war we didn't really know for sure whether our children in camp were dead or alive. We had to leave China, coming out via India, where we picked up our wee girlie, Dorothea, and we got on a troop ship to come home. We were a long, long time on that ship; every day seemed like a year.
>
> When we got to New York, I asked if any of the internees or prisoners of war had come that way. They said no. Well we got off that boat with heavy hearts. But a group of Red Cross workers approached us and called out "Is there a Mr. and Mrs. John Bell here?"
>
> I said "Yes, I'm Mrs. Bell." I picked up a letter quickly and opened it and found it was from Mr. Ernest Davis from the CIM in Philadelphia; "Dear John and Edith, You will be surprised to know that your children arrived home two days ago." I was completely overcome. My children not only came from the land of the enemy, they came to their own border as the verse in Jeremiah had promised. They came to Toronto.
>
> John and I got on a train that night, and what a long night it was for us! At last the porter came through the train and called out, "We are now in Ontario, Canada, and we will have a ten-minute stop in Hamilton." John said we must get off. After the train stopped we

stepped down and were almost knocked over by our three children, who had come to meet us. It was joy unspeakable and full of glory. God's "I wills" had not failed, and we knew they never would. The children came on board, and we all took the train back to Toronto together.

By late October 1945 the "Down Under" party, of which I was a part, boarded H.M.S. *Reaper,* a converted aircraft carrier bound for Sydney, Australia. We had a beautiful trip coming through the tropics, and by its end I wanted to join both the navy and the air force! Everyone was kindness itself to us wartime "orphans."

I was still finding it hard to resist the "scrounging" instinct that internment had bred in us. When I saw a whole pile of free Gideon New Testaments—with great self-control, I thought—I took only two, one of which I signed to register my recommitment to Christ as my Lord and Master.

On board I saw my first movie: "Meet Me in Saint Louis." It was an overwhelming experience; many of the scenes are still vividly etched on my memory to this day.

It was here, too, in the middle of the South China Sea, that I took another eagerly-awaited step toward freedom. Bright moonlight and calm seas had turned the night into a balmy paradise. I went to my cabin and hurried back up on deck with a bundle hidden under my arm. Here was my chance. The teachers wouldn't see me. I was alone on deck. The ship rose and dipped gently on the waves as I pulled out my secret bundle and with great feeling of relief, flung overboard my burden, the enamel potty that had accompanied me to my chagrin all those years. Close behind it came my one other piece of once-necessary equipment, now obsolete—my chipped enamel pie dish. I leaned over the railing and watched as they sank slowly beneath the waves. Gradually they disappeared from view, taking with them my last link with the hardship and imprisonment of the past six years. I wouldn't need them any more! It was a moment of celebration.

One other possession remained. It had followed me through all the Chefoo experience, and I was not going to part with it now. The box was broken, and a piece of string, "scrounged" with great difficulty, held it together. Inside, packed with painstaking care, lay my dominoes. Carefully I lifted the lid and traced my fingers over the dots again as I had when I first got them. Was it only six years ago I had opened them on the truck amid tears? Half a lifetime ago it was. For half my life my dominoes had been my one tangible link with home and parents. Now I was to see both. Would my parents have changed? Would I still remember them? And they me? After all I wasn't the same little boy they had given the dominoes to. I bent the sides of the box back into place for the hundredth time, tied them up carefully and put them back in my bag.

A comic sight we must have presented, lined up as we were in our many-sizes-too-big GI clothes, coming under the mighty Harbor Bridge into Sydney. Peering down from the giddy height of the flight deck, we scanned the wharf, desperately hoping for a glimmer of recognition. Neil Yorkston (today a psychiatrist in Vancouver), who came back on an earlier ship, was standing on the pier beside my Dad. He pointed out my sister and me under our GI caps, as we pressed against the rail.

Once the gangplank was down, my Dad came on board. Joyce rushed into his arms and I saw her heels flying in the air. I felt embarrassed and held back for a moment, but then ran forward with arms outstretched. The six to seven years of separation were over at last.

There was a welcome-home celebration for us in the Sydney

town hall, and then it was on to Adelaide, South Australia. The pilot of the RAF Dakota that flew us, having heard something of our story, let me sit in the copilot's seat and "fly" the plane a bit. "You might as well try this part of the war too," he said.

After we touched down at Parafield, it slowly dawned on us that we were together as a complete family for the first time. A new life began for the six of us. Joyce and I met our younger sister Joan again; and our younger brother Brian, who was nearly four, we saw for the first time.

A summer Christmas followed by vacation helped us to catch up with Western civilization. Then in February 1946 I started school—a real school, with proper desks and chairs and playing fields. My accent was very British, and the teacher advised the children to copy me. But I was more interested in copying *them*.

Classmates had difficulty believing some of the stories I told them. Only when I brought along some of my pieces of parachute—especially the piece signed by some of the GIs who dropped into Weihsien Camp—were they convinced. I had come out of another world.

Sometimes as I sat in class those first weeks at the Grange Primary School, my mind would wander back to Weihsien. Losing the teacher, I would look out of the window and see the trees, the neat houses and tidy fields, and in the far-off distance, the wide horizon and open sky. The walls were gone. I was free. I would burst into tears—tears of relief, of happiness and of thankfulness.

I had lived so much already and, after all, I was only just twelve years old. What could I do with all of my past experience? A whole wonderful future stretched out before me. I ran to it enthusiastically as I had run down that cinder track on sports day over a year before.

Yet there were some things from my past I would never leave behind. "Come on, Brian," I said to my brother whom I was gradually getting to know, "I'll teach you how to play dominoes."

> When the Lord brought back the captives to Zion,
> We were like men who dreamed.
> Our mouths were filled with laughter,
> Our tongues with songs of joy.
> Then it was said among the nations,
> "The Lord has done great things for them."
> The Lord has done great things for us,
> And we are filled with joy.
>
> Psalm 126, verses 1–3

Chapter 11

WEIHSIEN REVISITED

"What can a tired heart say,
Which the wise of the world have made dumb?
Save to the lonely dreams of a child, 'Return again, come!'"

—Walter De La Mare, *Dreams*

In the summer of 1981, thirty-six years after World War II had ended, John Hoyte and I were looking at each other across the table at the centenary celebration of the Chefoo School at the Holiday Inn in Toronto. I had moved with my wife Joan and our four children from Japan to Toronto in 1974 to take up the responsibility of Director of the Overseas Missionary Fellowship in Canada. Our conversation that day went back to the times when as boys we played marbles together in the dirt of Weihsien. We remembered those marbles matches which had helped us while away the waiting hours of the daily roll call, only to come to an abrupt end as angry boots appeared in front of our noses and our eyes followed them up into the glowering faces of the Japanese guards.

John and I were kindred spirits. Weihsien had also given him a love of adventure. One of his early post-China exploits had been to head up a student expedition, leading an elephant across the Alps to prove his theory of the route Hannibal had taken centuries before.[1] Just as an elephant never forgets, neither do Chefusians (Chefoo alumni). Now we dreamed about a new adventure—of some day returning to Weihsien. Since China was opening up again to tourists, we wondered out loud if we might perhaps get back there one of these years.

Some months later, as I sat with my family around the dining room table, I was surveying the scattered sections of the Saturday edition of the Toronto *Star*. The front-page headlines of the Entertainment section caught my eye. The subject was an Olympic athlete who wouldn't run on a Sunday and who finished by winning the gold medal.

Why, I thought, *that has to be Eric Liddell!* I quickly read on. Sure enough, it was Eric Liddell's story, and Warner Brothers, I discovered, had made a movie in Britain about the 1924 Olympics. The film was causing quite a stir, having been chosen for the Royal Command Performance in London. It was making its debut at a theater in Toronto that very day. Of course, our family all went. The standing ovation that greeted the end of the film was inspiring, but it was the lines about Eric Liddell that came onto the screen near the close that moved me to tears. My boyhood memories of Weihsien Camp all came flooding back as I read them: "Eric Liddell, missionary, died in occupied China at the end of World War II. All of Scotland mourned."

[1]John Hoyte, *Trunk Road for Hannibal* (London: Geoffrey Bles, 1960); reprint: *Alpine Elephant: In Hannibal's Tracks* (Palo Alto, California: Fabrizio Publications, 1975).

The next weekend I was very surprised to find an interview and picture of Florence Liddell Hall, Eric Liddell's widow, on the front page of the newspaper. I had forgotten that Florence was a Canadian, and in any case, I thought that she and the family had settled in Scotland after the war.

I never imagined that she was still living. But it didn't take me long to find her telephone number through the directory service and to discover that she was living in Binbrook, near Hamilton, only about an hour from Toronto. I dialed the number with my heart pounding, and when Florence answered, I said, "You won't know me, but I was a boy in Weihsien Camp." I paused as the line was quiet and then continued, "Eric used to referee our soccer games and look after us every Thursday afternoon to give our teachers a break. He was Uncle Eric to us. In fact, he was more like a father to us younger children separated from our parents."

When Florence found words to reply, she said, "Oh! I can't believe it. This is wonderful. Can you come and visit me?"

And visit I did, taking with me Gordon Martin, my old Latin teacher at Chefoo, who had moved from England to rural Ontario some years before. What a moving afternoon we had as we talked with Florence and two of her daughters, Patricia and Heather, recalling memory after memory! Gordon had worked with Eric on the Sports and Education committees in Weihsien. I brought out treasured photos, tattered Red Cross letters, and pieces of parachute. Florence told us with tears in her eyes that she didn't get the news of Eric's death until nearly three months after he had gone. "His last letter was dated the day he died, February 21, 1945, and didn't reach me until the end of May," she whispered.

One week before the Academy Awards were to be presented in 1981 Florence and I were interviewed on "W-5"—a half-hour Canadian T.V. show dealing with current events. We had a chance to answer questions, share recollections, and also give clear testimony to God's grace. The hosts of the program told the viewers it was their prediction that the film was the "dark horse" and would win an Oscar. They were right, of course. When "Chariots of Fire" won the Academy Award for Best Picture, Florence and her family as well as Christians around the world were thrilled. Eric Liddell's achievements had given glory to God one more time.

With the dawning of 1985 John Hoyte and I realized that August 17 would mark the fortieth anniversary of our rescue from Weihsien Camp. We wrote a letter or two back and forth. I told him of other plans I had to be in Asia in the fall, and we began to dream. An adventure was taking shape in our minds. We would go together to China that August and be at Weihsien right on the anniversary of our rescue—the day when forty years before, the seven GIs dropped out of the sky ending our imprisonment.

John wrote Arthur Hummel, former escapee of Weihsien, who at that time was the American Ambassador to China. John told him of our idea and suggested we might meet him there. Hummel replied that, as he would be on home leave in August, he would unhappily miss our visit.

Plans gradually came together, however. John would take his fourteen-year-old son, Jonathan, and I would take Ken, our sixteen-year-old. Then, just weeks before we left, John's sister, Mary Broughton, and her thirteen-year-old son, James, decided to join us. Two Chinese-speaking OMF missionaries, Don Houliston and Cyril Weller, made our party complete. A junior missionary to my parents, Cyril had seen me off to Chefoo from Kweiyang in 1939.

We took with us a commemorative plaque on which we had had inscribed the following:

This plaque is presented by the CIM Chefoo Schools Association
to commemorate with deep gratitude
the fortieth anniversary of the liberation
of 1400 prisoners, including some 500 children,
from Weihsien Internment Camp
by 7 American GI's on August 17, 1945,
at the end of World War II.
The last resting place of Eric Liddell,
Olympic hero of "Chariots of Fire,"
who died in the Camp February 21, 1945.

Below was an embossed picture of Eric Liddell and our names and the date.

On August 14 our party of eight, having all safely converged on Hong Kong, flew to Beijing. The Chinese wherever we went were extremely friendly, and the international mix of our team intrigued them. Between us we represented Canada, U.S.A., England, Australia, New Zealand, South Africa, and China, of course, as three of us had been born there.

Without Don Houliston organizing our travel and accommodation as we journeyed, I doubt if we would have survived, as August is China's busiest and hottest month. We made the most of our short visit in Beijing, seeing Tiananmen Square and other places. From there we also visited the Great Wall.

An amazing experience was that on our first bus ride into the city, we found ourselves close to a university student who was very outgoing and spoke fluent English. In a loud voice he said to us, "I am very interested in philosophy and relygion (religion)," and as he said this, he put his hands together as one would when praying.

We looked around the bus packed full of passengers and quietly replied, "We're very interested in religion too."

After further conversation, I very quietly showed him a little Chinese booklet which I had in my bag, entitled, "What is Christianity?" and asked him if he would like to have it. He nodded enthusiastically, and I slipped it into his hand.

I was surprised to see that he didn't put it out of sight immediately but began to look at it, as did some of the other people around him. Communist antipathy to religion seemed to be diminishing, we concluded. We told him that we were going on to Chefoo and Weihsien in Shandong Province. These places are now called Yantai and Weifang. Imagine our surprise when this young man told us that Weifang was his home town! He had attended the middle school which was not far from our former camp.

We took the night train, and reached Yantai (Chefoo) at 4:30 the next morning. It was Sunday, and already the city was very much alive with the ubiquitous bicycle and pedestrian traffic. We were able to get into the new Chinese Overseas Guests Hotel, which, we discovered to our delight, was less than half a mile above the old Chefoo School property.

While high-rise apartments below the hotel made it difficult to see much of the old compound, later on in the morning, after attending the open church on Victory Road, we walked down to the boardwalk on the beach. After walking along the boardwalk—known to us as the "Bund"—we came to the end of the concrete breakwater wall and went down onto the sand. We ran across the sandy stretch, through the crowds enjoying the hot weather and the swimming. It was the same beach where we swam as six- and seven-year-olds in the early 40s. Over at the left of the bay the Bluff looked just the same, and in the middle distance we could see the clear lines of Lighthouse Island.

As we turned to walk inland, all of a sudden, right in front of us, we saw it again—our old school compound. A lot of new buildings, including restaurants, had been built right on the shore, but there to our right was the old boat shed and in front of us the main gate—it was a much bigger one than the old one—and stretching away to the right was the old Boys' School wall. Suddenly it was as if it were 1942 again, and I was seeing my school heroes, the twelfth-graders (sixth formers in the British system), staggering past us as they came to the end of the Long Run while we Prepites were propped up on the wall cheering them on.

We were able to go upstairs in the new restaurant on the beach and got a good view of the Co-Ed Building, the Memorial Hall, and in between the two, a section of the Prep School.

Two of us did our best to get into the compound, but since the whole area has been taken over as a naval base, we were soon stopped by a marine on guard. At least we got our feet onto Chefoo School soil. We retreated sluggishly, as I tried to crane my neck to see around the bend of the main road into the compound. I wanted to get at least a glimpse of the front door of the Prep School where, at the age of six, I had taken my last stand on the school steps. But we were told to move away and reluctantly had to comply.

We sat down outside the gate and lost ourselves in contemplation. I remembered that moment of struggle all too clearly. But then I pictured myself a few years later coming out of that gate in marching column with the Japanese soldiers barking out orders against the background of clanging swords and rifles. In my mind's eye I saw us then trudging off to Temple Hill for internment.

Out of the blue a voice beside me interrupted my reverie to ask in English, "Can you speak Japanese?"

"Japanese!" I exclaimed. *"Hai, dekimasu"* ("Yes, I can"). Soon we were talking nonstop in Japanese. My new-found Chinese friend was a engineering student at the university. He was learning Japanese, as he was very keen to go to Japan.

It was almost uncanny—over forty years later—to be sitting outside my old school and talking Japanese at that. I found myself telling him my life story, beginning with the first sight of the Japanese soldiers entering the very gateway in front of us. I recounted how I learned Japanese numbers and spent the war years in captivity in China.

Telling my story was severely taxing my rusty Japanese, but he wanted me to go on with it. I told him how I came to give my life to God and how real God's love was to me. I told him that after I had been a high-school teacher for a few years, I had left Australia at the age of 26 and had worked as a missionary in Japan for ten years.

He was puzzled. "But, what is a missionary? Tell me, what did you actually *do?*"

I replied that I had taught English and the Bible to university students and that as I made friends with the students and also the people in our neighborhood where we lived, we explained the way to come to know God and His love.

Since my new Chinese friend was in no hurry to leave, I told him about one particular Japanese student, Mr. Makino. Makino-san had been a Buddhist but became a Christian while he was a student and later on went as a missionary to Thailand to teach young people the Bible. My Chinese friend seemed to listen very eagerly.

Typhoon winds that were gathering over the sea soon caught our attention. Noticing the sky was growing darker by the minute, we knew the time had come to say *"Sayonara."*

Our party walked round behind the school into what we had known as "Mule Road." Here we had a good view of many of the other buildings, which were now used by the naval forces. Since we didn't want to get caught in the storm, we knew we had to hurry, but we were loath to leave. We drew ourselves away reluctantly, looking back frequently over our shoulders in the direction of the school, while at the same time, glancing nervously forward and upward to the sky.

An elderly man wheeling his bicycle came up alongside us. He spoke in good English and volunteered the information that he remembered the days when teachers, missionaries, and children were housed on the compound. The war and all the bombing and the suffering were something he could never forget. Then, to my further amazement, he switched languages, and we carried on the conversation in Japanese. For me to be met with such associations of Japan there at Chefoo was like a rendezvous with the past.

We awoke the next morning to find ourselves enveloped in a typhoon, of an intensity unequaled in the last thirty-five years in that region. A "breaking-up" storm-and-a-half had come to welcome us back to Chefoo. The fierce winds uprooted trees, sent towering waves crashing over the breakwater, sinking or wrecking more than 200 ships, and damaging 25,000 homes. Further north, torrential rains and hail the size of grapefruit wreaked more devastation.

In the afternoon, when the weather eased a little, we managed to get up to Temple Hill. Because the Presbyterian Mission buildings just below had been taken over by the military, we were not able to go into what had been the first place of our school internment. Nonetheless, we were able to see two of the three buildings and, with much nostalgia, to take pictures.

A number of soldiers were standing around at Temple Hill.
The soldier standing by the main gate gave me a start. Except
for the different uniform and the fact that it was over forty
years later, I thought for a moment that I was looking at Major
Kosaka again!

Before we left Chefoo I looked out from the hotel balcony
over the apartments below and saw the tops of our old school
buildings. I thought of the educational and spiritual heights to
which our teachers had encouraged us to aspire. Indeed, Gordon Martin, our classics teacher, must have influenced more
than just the school. There on the clock face in the hotel lobby,
I saw in small print *"Tempus Fugit."* I smiled. It seemed appropriate that if there is any place in China one can see Latin, it
should be in Chefoo, where "Goopy" had left his mark.

Our two days at Chefoo had simply flown. Close to midnight
on August 16 we boarded the train for Weifang. A diesel, the
train was packed with people and made frequent stops. Though
the six of us who had soft berths got a bit more sleep than the
two on the hard berths, we all got a lot more sleep than we
would have on the seats.

With what excitement we pulled into Weifang just
after midday on August 17! This was the day we
had been waiting for. Gone were the high city
walls, and the new station bore no resemblance to the one we
had come into with fear and trepidation in the dark days of the
war. Nor did we have to scramble for luggage thrown out the
window in a two-minute frenzy before being herded onto
trucks. Instead, Mr. Li of the Department of Foreign Affairs
came with a mini-van to meet us at the station, since we had
written to inform him of our mission.

After a Chinese meal, we boarded the van from the Weifang

Hotel for the Second Middle School, our old camp. What were open fields in our time were now roads and houses. The high walls were mostly gone, and our camp was almost indistinguishable from the city that had now overtaken it.

In no time, it seemed, after traveling only a relatively short distance, the mini-van stopped, and we got out. Close by was a large, foreign-looking building where the present school staff had their rooms. Momentarily we were disoriented. Then we realized we were looking at one of the original Presbyterian missionary homes, which had been out of bounds to us, as it was where the Japanese had their headquarters during the war years. "Of course," we chuckled, "it's the place where the guards tried to keep Father Scanlan after his egg-smuggling exploits." I turned to look ahead, still a bit dazed; forty years were cascading over me. We had entered from what had been the back of Weihsien Camp in our time. Then, all of a sudden, it all but overwhelmed me—there ahead of us stood Block 23 in all its faded glory. The bell tower in the middle of the building was mostly gone, but the rest of the building looked much the same, except more dilapidated.

Mr. Wei, the principal, invited us to the staff room, where Mr. Wong, the vice-principal, and an interpreter joined us. As we sipped Chinese tea and ate watermelon, the principal told us something of the history of the school. He knew it was begun in 1883. Then, when it was our turn, we spoke a little about our experiences during the war and presented on behalf of the Chefoo Schools Association the commemorative plaque that we had brought with us. They sensed the significance of the visit for us with our sons, particularly as we were there on this special anniversary of the day the seven GIs had parachuted down. How we wished that Jimmy Moore, a fellow Chefoo graduate who was one of the parachutists, could have been with us!

The principal said that they would mount the plaque behind glass in a suitable place in the school for students and visitors to see. He wanted to learn more about our experiences through the war and read the story of Eric Liddell's life.

We walked out of the building and down towards Block 23. Unfortunately, we couldn't go inside because the building was in a bad state of disrepair. We heard with some sadness that it would be demolished before too long. I went to the right end of the building and managed to peek through the keyhole and saw the places round the little room where we had slept on the floor during our years of internment.

"That's where I slept," I called to Ken. "And there's where the others were—Paul Grant, Philip Paulson, John Taylor, Val Nicholls, Ray Moore, John Birch, Robert Clow, and David Allen." For a brief moment I thought quietly of John Birch, killed in a motorcyle accident while studying to become a medical missionary at the University of British Columbia in the early 1950s. I tried to peer into the room alongside, where our teachers had lived. It seemed just like yesterday that Miss Carr, Miss Stark, Miss Woodward, Miss Priestman, and Miss Young had been there. Across the narrow hall was the smaller room where the Prep School girls had stayed.

I walked around outside and saw the windows out of which we had sometimes climbed in the dead of night to take our Tom Sawyer-like trips round the camp in the hot summer months. Peering in through the pasted-over windows, I saw where our trunks had been lined up on the floor in the middle. Looking up, I was astounded to see behind piled-up boxes the same old blackboard still hanging on the wall, just where it had been in 1945.

As we walked slowly down past the long row of huts, it was like being on holy ground. We passed the one where the Martin family had lived, and then on to what used to be our soccer- or ball-field. My heart sank as I saw that a big factory had swallowed up almost all the open space. On the right, where the old Edwardian church had been, another large building had been constructed.

We stood on the little remaining piece of our old field, close to the front wall of the camp. Gone were the searchlight towers and the electrified and barbed wire, but the sky above was the same. For a brief moment we looked up and thought of "The Armored Angel" as it flew in low and sent down our liberators exactly forty years before.

Across that same sky modern jets from a military base not far away streaked by with a deafening roar, bringing us back rudely to reality.

Going on a bit farther, we came to the front wall and it felt good to lean on it. We stopped to look over. Beyond the wall there was no sign of the straggling little village, nor any trace of the old garbage pit that every day used to swallow up from our sight the scavenging Chinese children as they desperately searched for something edible among the scraps thrown out from Weihsien Camp. Between the newer houses and low walls, I caught a glimpse of the little stream that ran close to the old path along which we had run when we first welcomed the GIs. Further in the distance were tall blocks of apartments covering the once open fields where our food from heaven had floated down.

Carefully, almost religiously, I pulled from my pocket a packet of Chiclets that I had specially brought with me. I slowly savored one as I thought back to the days when, ravenously, I tore open a food parcel and relished my first taste of the mystery candy, chewing gum.

Our hosts kept us moving, though we were loath to leave.

We wished time would stand still for a while. Our sons looked on quizzically as they saw us contemplating past memories.

We weren't able to get through to the hospital side of the camp because of walls that had been built up, dividing the hospital from the school. However, we saw a little of some of the other large buildings and the old kitchen and then, after going out to the main street, were able to come in at the entrance of the new hospital. Here the school staff passed us over to the head doctor, Dr. Shia, who spoke very good English, and we where shown over the other part of our old camp, which included Shadyside Hospital, known as Block 61 during internment. Dr. Shia showed us some sections of the new 600-bed hospital which now adjoins the old camp hospital.

What was once the basketball court close by was now littered with rubble. We paused beside it, close to the place where Brian Thompson had been electrocuted during roll call, and then looked just beyond to see the older part of the hospital and the room where Eric Liddell had died. We looked at each other and saw ourselves for an instant, as we were forty years before, standing in line at attention as part of the honor guard, forming the pathway to the grave outside.

At the front of the hospital the name, "Shadyside Hospital" had been almost obliterated through the efforts of the Red Guards in the 1960s in their fanaticism to wipe out evidence of Western culture and the Christian faith. A little further away was the long hut in one room of which Herbert Taylor had lived. Here Jim Taylor had sometimes stayed with his grandfather.

We looked up at the top of the hospital, and although we didn't have time to go in, as we were quite closely shepherded, we saw the windows of the attic floors where the Boys' and Girls' School had stayed. Suddenly Mary called out, "There's the old water tower!" and we all took pictures of that too.

If the old water tower could have spoken, what stories it could have told of secret rendezvous, of boys pumping by the hour day after day, or of mischievous Prepites hiding in its dark recesses to boil up their bread-porridge in little beat-up cans or to fry rusk-like bread in peanut oil, producing fried bread, one of the gourmet menu items of camp.

Finally, I looked in vain for any sign of the little camp grave-yard. The humble mound of earth and simple wooden cross with Eric H. Liddell written with shoe-blacking on the cross-piece had long since gone. Large blocks of apartments now obscured the site. But in my searching I found a lovely garden with an ornamental gate behind it. I envisaged that this was where the wasted pallbearers had stopped in their solemn task as we had watched them bear the simple coffin from camp.

Night was falling, and our visit was nearing its end. In the distance, our train signaled its approach. But we made no attempt to leave; we were reliving the struggles and sufferings of the past—the agony of the inner battles and the anguish of the outer War.

I walked forward and stood among the flowers. For a few brief moments I was oblivious of those around me, and for yet one more time, I was a boy again, living with my heroes. I fell to my knees and gave thanks to God—thanks for faith and His abiding faithfulness and for freedom no walls can contain.

China Inland Mission Missionaries and Children Interned by the Japanese at Weihsien

Of the more than 1,400 internees in Weihsien Concentration Camp, 253 were connected with the China Inland Mission. They comprised the children in the Chefoo Schools, staff and families, and a few other missionaries, both active and retired.

FROM CHEFOO
CIM SCHOOL STAFF AND FAMILIES

BRITISH (from the U.K., Canada, Australia, New Zealand, S. Africa)

Barling, Mrs. Lily
    John

Bazire, Mr. and Mrs. Reg V.
    Theo
    Peter

Brayne, Miss Mary L.

Broomhall, Mrs. A. Hudson

Broomhall, Miss E. Marjory

Bruce, Mr. and Mrs. Pat A.
    James
    Jean

Burn, Miss E. Florence

Carr, Miss Ailsa K.

Chalkley, Mr. and Mrs. Harold J.
    Betty
    Mary
    Donovan
    Ann

Cobb, Miss Doris B.

Davey, Miss Evelyn G.

Dobson, Miss Rita I. M.

Faers, Mr. and Mrs. A. H.

Fraser, Mrs. Roxie
    Catherine
    Dorothy
    Margaret

Graham, Mr. and Mrs. John

Greening, Miss Ruth E.

Hanna, Mrs. Cora*
    Grant*
    Bruce*
    Roxie*

Harris, Mr. and Mrs. Reg F.
    Isabel
    Maida

Henderson, Miss Hettie G.

Hills, Miss Jeanie E.

Houghton, Mr. and Mrs. Stanley
    Stephen
    Felicity
    Josephine

Howie, Dr. and Mrs. A. Hallam
    David
    Ivan
    Margaret (born in Weihsien)

Jennings, Mr. and Mrs. Alfred

Jennings, Miss Jessie W.

Jackson, Mr. and Mrs. Gerald B.
    Margaret
    Peter

King, Mrs. Ivy
    Comfort (Irene)
    Joy

CIM SCHOOL STAFF AND FAMILIES (cont.)

BRITISH (from the U.K., Canada, Australia, New Zealand, S. Africa) cont.

Lack, Mrs. Beatrice
  Jean
  Henry
  Handley
Lucia, Miss Ina T.
Mann, Miss M. Carrie
Martin, Mr. and Mrs. S. Gordon
  Elizabeth
  John
  Alison
  Richard
Mason, Mrs. Hannah J.
Neve, Dr. Helen R.
Olesen, Mr. and Mrs. Peter O.
Phare, Miss Inez E.
Priestman, Miss Monica G.
Pyle, Miss Margaret
Seaman, Mr. and Mrs. Roy A.
  Doris
  Grace
Stark, Miss Bea M.
Taylor, Mr. Herbert Hudson
Taylor, Miss Isabel J.
Taylor, Mr. and Mrs. William
Thompson, Mrs. Ella
  Brian (died in Weihsien Camp)
  Paul
  Stanley
  Joan
Welch, Mr. and Mrs. Gordon P.
  Sylvia
  Beryl
  Theodore
  Bernard

Warren, Mr. and Mr. S. J.
  Catherine
  Allison
  David
Windsor, Mrs. T. (died in Weihsien Camp)
Williams, Miss Leila M.
Willoughby, Miss A. Kathleen
Woodward, Miss Dorothy E.
Young, Miss Pearl G.

AMERICAN

Andrews, Mr. & Mrs. H. E. V.*
Fitzwilliam, Mrs. Jenny*
  John*
Hess, Mrs. Esther*
Philips, Miss Martha H.*
Smail, Mrs. Alma*
  Kathleen*
  Ian*
Thomas, Mrs. Ruth*
  Rhoda Jeanne*
  David*

NORWEGIAN

Torjesen, Mrs. Wallberg
  Kari
  Haakon
  Torje

CIM CHILDREN SEPARATED FROM PARENTS

BRITISH (from the
U.K., Canada, Australia,
New Zealand, S. Africa)

Allen, David
Amos, Paul
  Helen
Andrews, John
  George
  Dorothy
  Mabel
Beard, David
Bell, John*
  Agnes
  George
  Edith
  Mary*
  Ruth
  Kenneth
Bevan, Marian
  Audrey
  Jennifer
Birch, David
  John
Binks, Evelyn
  Thomas
  Alfred
  Mabel
Cliff, Norman
  Lelia
  Estelle
Clow, Jean
  Robert
Edwards, Elizabeth
Graham, Jack
  Enid
Grant, Paul
Goodwin, Stewart
  Joanna

Harrison, James
  Marjorie
Hayman, Andrew
  Frances
  Ben
Hoyte, Robin
  Eric
  Rupert
  Mary
  John
  Elizabeth
Jones, Richard
Keeble, Bruce
Kerry, Joyce
  Brian
Knight, Dorothy
Learner, Margaret
Liversidge, Grace
Longden, Ramsay
Martin, Christine
Maxwell, Joy
Metcalf, Stephen
Michell, Joyce
  David
Moore, Raymond
Nicholls, Valwynne
Patchett, Kenneth
  Betty
Paulson, Philip
Reimer, Alexander
Sadler, Douglas
  Murray
Savage, Gordon
Scott, Margaret
  Basil
Slade, Ronald
  Nora

Stedeford, Roland
Strange, Kathleen
  Beryl
Taylor, Kathleen
  James
  Mary
  John
Trickey, Clifford
  Raymond
  Doris
  Irene
Vinden, Margaret
  Dick
Windsor, Marjory
Yorkston, Neil
Young, James
  Joan
  Margaret

AMERICAN

Beckon, Fronsie*
Cooke, Joseph*
Desterhaft, Wallace*
  Alvin*
Englund, Winifred*
Harris, Frederick*
Hatton, Betty*
  Howard*
  John*
Hulse, Barbara*
  Hugh*
Kohfield, Bernice*
  Bruce*
  Byron*
Kuhn, Kathryn*

AMERICAN (cont.)	NORWEGIAN	DUTCH
Nowack, Mary Pearl*	Nordmo, Stanley	Costerus, Raymond
Phillips, Richard*	Kathleen	Chris
Kathryn*	Audrey	Helen

FROM TSINGTAO

CIM MISSIONARIES AND CHILDREN

Whipple, Mr. and Mrs. Elden C.*   Walton, Mr. and Mrs. Nathan E.*
    Elden*   Barbara*
    Lorna*   Nathan Thomas*
    Dwight*   Lois (Lindie)*
    Julie*

The 47 people marked with an asterisk (*) were repatriated from Weihsien September 19, 1943. They left for North America on the *S. S. Gripsholm.* The following CIM missionaries and child were also repatriated on the *Gripsholm*, leaving from Shanghai:

Foucar, Miss Dorothea M., R.N.   Olson, Lawrence
Gemmell, Miss Nina E.   Pflueger, Miss Lydia E.
Hill, Mrs. Marie   Robinson, Miss Laura J.
    Doris   Simpson, Miss Marjorie I.
Lederach, Miss Kathryn   Swarr, Miss Anna K.

"A Boy's War" is a good look at what it meant to be a missionary child trusting God in the presence of many enemies. It presents the dedication and practical working out of faith in the midst of difficulties; of serving Jesus as Lord and Savior regardless of the circumstances.

Too often in modern presentations of the "Good News" we forget to mention the bad news. Hard times will come if you are a Christian! Count on it! You've just read about how a group of Christians experienced the faithfulness of God. There was, in this story, no plea that you should become a Christian, but know full well that there is a hell. Know too, that our works, good as they may seem, will not let us escape. Even man's best does not reach far above the atrocities of war and greed.

The Bible tells us that "all have sinned" (Romans 3:23), there are no exceptions. It also tells us that the "wages of sin is death" (Romans 6:23) meaning that the payment, the reward for our sinful lives is eternal condemnation and separation from God. Truly a bleak picture were it not for the familiar and glorious promise that "whoever believes in Him (Jesus) should not perish but have eternal life." (John 3:16)

Only Jesus can save us. He desires to know us completely, and loves us in spite of our failures. He is willing to make us become holy like Himself. The biggest war any one of us will face will not be a battle toward "flesh and blood, but against principalities, against powers, against the rulers of darkness ..." (Ephesians 6:12) Only with Jesus can we win not only the daily battles, but ultimately the war to end all wars, your eternal life.

This copy of "A Boy's War" has been distributed as a "thank-you" for your purchase from The Timberdoodle and was made possible by Overseas Missionary Fellowship. We hope that your family and friends have been challenged by its message.

May God continue to bless your family.

Dan, Deb
Joy, Hope, Grace, Abel and Pearl

Timberdoodle Company - E 1510 Spencer Lake Rd. - Shelton, WA 98584